RAW TALKS WITH WISDOM

MIKE PASCHALL

NOT YOUR GRANDMA'S DEVO

volume 2
APRIL, MAY, JUNE

RAW TALKS WITH WISDOM - Not Your Grandma's Devo
Volume 2 - (April, May, & June).

Copyright © 2013, 2018 by Michael D. Paschall.

All rights reserved. No part of this book may be reproduced or stored in a retrieval system, or transmitted in any form or by any means—electronic, mechanical, photocopying, recording, or otherwise, without the written permission of owner.

FIRST EDITION

ISBN: 978-0-578-42653-2

Cover & Title Page: Jon C. Egan

EVERY TRIBE INTERNATIONAL
Colorado Springs, Colorado

www.everytribeinternational.org
mike@mikepaschall.com

CONTENTS

Preface   v

Dedication   ix

APRIL   1 - 50

MAY   53 - 102

JUNE   105 - 154

Endnotes   157

Resources & Other Helps   159

Acknowledgements   163

Author   167

PREFACE

HEY! Thank you so much for giving ***RAW TALKS WITH WISDOM – Not Your Grandma's Devo*** a whirl! It's an honor and a blessing to have you along for the ride. Before we get started, I thought it would be helpful to give you an idea of what this thing is all about.

FOUNDATIONS

Setting aside time every day for a devotional is probably one of the best disciplines I was ever encouraged to implement into my daily life. It has provided me countless connections with the Lord.

For the past 35 years, I have primarily read devotionals by two men, Dr. James Sidlow Baxter and Oswald Chambers. I was introduced to Dr. Baxter in 1978 by my first real spiritual mentor: Dr. H. D. McCarty. I heard Brother Sidlow speak on more than one occasion. He was already in his late '70s by the time I was introduced to his written work. I will always be thankful for **AWAKE MY HEART**. I learned so much from the meditations in that devotional.

Our friends, Earl and Barbara Patrick, gave me my first copy of **MY UTMOST FOR HIS HIGHEST** by Oswald Chambers when I was ordained in April 1986. I still use that same copy. I can't begin to describe the blessing that devotional has been to me. Chambers' revelations are amazing, especially considering he was only 43 years old when he died in 1917. His wife, Biddy, compiled transcripts and notes that eventually evolved into **UTMOST**, first published in 1927. I am forever in debt to them both for what was spoken, captured, and put into print for all of us to benefit.

MY DESIRE

My prayer is that the Lord will speak to you through ***RAW TALKS WITH WISDOM – Not Your Grandma's Devo***. I have always gained wisdom and perspective by reading scripture and devotionals, but more important to me has been how the Holy Spirit tailors each lesson to fit my life. It doesn't really mean anything unless we can practically apply truth to the joys and tears of the now.

If all you come away with after working through these devotionals is more knowledge, then I'd have to really evaluate if it was all worth it. I would encourage you to take it to another level, beyond mere theology and theory, into the realms of practical reality—stuff you can wear, taste, and feel. I want you to know He gave you revelation!

MY VISION

It's simple. Do this devotional the way you would do any other devotional. But what I really want is for these daily lessons to stimulate journaling (which is the reason for the **"In the Pages"** questions at the end of each day). I would encourage you to make an appointment to meet with the Lord each day, and then stick with it. Daily appointments can become healthy habits in a relatively short period of time. Pick a time each day that "works" best for you, and make Him a priority!

I want the material to stick with you. I want you to chew on it throughout your day. I want you to discuss it over coffee with a friend or colleague. Stuff like that. My ultimate prayer is that ***RAW TALKS WITH WISDOM – Not Your Grandma's Devo*** adds value to your quiet times with the Lord!

Like I said, I want you to do this devotional the way you do devotionals. But here is the method I would use to tackle each day:

First, read the **entire chapter** of Proverbs for that day. If the day is June 11, then read all of Proverbs chapter 11.

Then read the focus verses that begin each devo.

Third, read the devotional itself.

Fourth, journal your responses to the **In The Pages** questions at the end, along with anything else you feel compelled to write about. Get yourself a good leather-bound journal! Your thoughts and prayers deserve a proper container.

Lastly, spend some time in prayer and meditation.

That is the vision.

I sincerely hope the Holy Spirit will speak to you through these devotionals and give you things to write about in your journal. I also hope these devotionals will get you in the habit of reading through all of Proverbs twelve times in one year. For as long as I have been soaking in Proverbs, I have found a surprise almost every time! A new perspective, a nugget of value, something I've never seen before. It has to be the Holy Spirit that does that, and so far, I love the process!

WHY *RAW TALKS WITH WISDOM* – *Not Your Grandma's Devo*?

It dawned on me one day that our relationships with the Lord should always be raw. I was stuck in the rut of religious activity for far too long! What I have with Him now feels very real, relaxed, and extremely relevant.

I live and work in a culture that is filled with young and old ideas. I have definitely mellowed over the years and learned how to slow down. I think this season is teaching me to be more focused on the stuff that actually counts. To say it, whatever "it" really is, without apology and with serious conviction.

I'm not a theologian. I know that. So there is no use in my trying to be one. I'm a weird mixture of stuff with a rich experience of failure and profound grace. ***RAW TALKS WITH WISDOM – Not Your Grandma's Devo*** is a title that feels like me. It gives me permission to be myself and say things like I really do.

I know the angels won't sing along to every single one of these devotionals for you. But maybe, just maybe, some of it will help someone, somewhere, turn and embrace the **RAW** truth of God's wisdom.

Michael D. Paschall
2013

For those who follow.

x

Too Late

April 1
Proverbs 1

"Since you laugh at my counsel and make a joke of my advice, how can I take you seriously? I'll turn the tables and joke about your troubles! What if the roof falls in, and your whole life goes to pieces? What if catastrophe strikes and there's nothing to show for your life but rubble and ashes? You'll need me then. You'll call for me, but don't expect an answer. No matter how hard you look, you won't find me." Proverbs 1:25-28, MSG

Solomon has burst into prophetic flow. The tachometer is pegged. This is no "April Fools" joke. The man has passion about what he is talking about here.

It is important to remember that he is referencing Lady Wisdom, NOT God. As the King often does, he personifies and dresses wisdom with quite an attitude. Sassy and real, almost frustrated with having all kinds of help and insight to offer, but no one is paying attention.

The prophets were familiar with this kind of language. God often spoke messages through them about His frustration with a rebellious, deaf-eared and idolatry prone Israel (Psalms 107:11; Isaiah 65:2, 12; Isaiah 66:4; Jeremiah 7:13; Zechariah 7:11).

Wisdom is suggesting there are serious consequences to not cashing in on what is made available to us. Peterson really softens the language here. I'm actually glad he does. Read it in the NASB or the NIV. It's B-R-U-T-A-L.

The overall message is pretty clear and fairly simple. When you have your chance to seek Lady Wisdom's help, do not waste the opportunity. She will respond with gracious help!

Also, understand that if you ignore her and act in foolishness, you'll reap a harvest from that folly, and nothing you do to try and make up for it will do you any good. It will be too late.

The seeds of foolishness bring fruits of foolishness. There is no way to undo the natural consequences with spiritual processes.

Policemen are trained to withstand verbal abuse and insults without reacting. They are not allowed to respond emotionally, no matter how intense or difficult the situation. Outbursts and/or profiling of any kind are simply not tolerated. They are entrusted to carry out and defend the laws of this land, and with that trust comes a huge responsibility.

"To Serve and Protect" is the motto of most police forces in America. We pay them to do just that. They are the preservers of peace... your peace... my peace. We need them.

I can read a speed limit sign. I know most of the rules for driving. Stop signs are in place for a reason. Wearing a seat belt is not optional. Whenever I'm not paying attention to these things, unpleasant yet perfectly reasonable consequences are to be expected.

It's a normal response to hit the brakes when we see a hidden patrol car. But by then, it's too late. The radar gun has clocked our speed long before we can do anything about it. So, we pray. We might get mercy, but most of the time, we rightfully pay.

Lady Wisdom really does want to "Serve and Protect". She is not a controller. She is a helper. We need to slow down and pay attention, before it's too late.

In The Pages

What is your emotional response to the seemed threats of wisdom in today's passage? Is "threats" the right word? Do you see the logic in what wisdom is forecasting?

Enter

April 2
Proverbs 2

"For wisdom will enter your heart, and moral knowledge will be attractive to you." Proverbs 2:10, NET

"So there remains a Sabbath rest for the people of God. For the one who has entered His rest has himself also rested from his works, as God did from His. Therefore let us be diligent to enter that rest, so that no one will fall, through following the same example of disobedience. For the word of God is living and active and sharper than any two-edged sword, and piercing as far as the division of soul and spirit, of both joints and marrow, and able to judge the thoughts and intentions of the heart. And there is no creature hidden from His

sight, but all things are open and laid bare to the eyes of Him with whom we have to do." Hebrews 4:9-13, NASB

Usually, anything I read in scripture that includes the word *"heart"* has my immediate attention. The **lêb** (pronounced *labe)* was the center of everything: mind (intellect and reason), will (fortitude and drive), emotion (love, hate, anger), care (forgiveness and mercy) and courage (internal strength).

Solomon believed that wisdom also needed to be at the center of man. Wisdom was to be a guiding strength that anchored us in truth and peace. When it is in its proper and rightful place inside of our DNA, it even affects our desires and appetites. Our passion for pleasing Him with moral rightness is stimulated and maintained by Lady Wisdom.

I am also attracted to the word *"enter,"* which also appears in today's text. The Hebrew word is **bôw'** (pronounced *bo).* There are a wide variety of applications, but it primarily means "*to come and go or abide."*

I have always known and believed that one of the biggest differences between the Judaic-Christian faith and all the others is the locale of spiritual transaction for man.

Much religious thought is about the discipline of the mind that infects and moderates moral behavior. Christ told us, over and over, that God is not fooled by our external performances. The real transactions are all sourced from inside of our heart (Matthew 23:26).

Right behavior is good.

Right behavior that flows from internal heart change is better!

Our mind is definitely involved (Romans 12:2), but it isn't all about our just deciding. The Spirit comes in and abides, blows on and changes our heart, intent, desire and mind, resulting in a different kind of life expression.

The writer of Hebrews says it beautifully in today's text, *"let us be diligent to enter into that rest."* Enter what rest? The rest in knowing that Christ has accomplished everything necessary for us to be at peace with God!

By the atonement of His blood we are washed clean and made whole. We are adopted "in" as sons and daughters of God. We don't have to keep the old rules, laws, and rituals to be accepted by God!

HE loves us, inhabits us, fills us, sanctifies us, and will one day glorify us! It's all done! Saying "yes" allows Him to *enter* and change it all from the inside out!

In The Pages

When did He enter your heart? What kind of assurance do you have about that? What has changed about you since then?

Why Be Like That?

April 3
Proverbs 3

"Do not withhold good from those to whom it is due, when it is in the power of your hand to do so. Do not say to your neighbor, "Go, and come back, and tomorrow I will give it," when you have it with you." Proverbs 3:27-28, NKJV

The NKJV says this the way it needs to be said. For those of us who truly have a desire to live out and manifest new covenant reality, graceful generosity should be a keystone passion of our heart.

Verse 27 instructs us to be faithful to pay and do what we promised. If we have hired someone to do a job for us, we need to pay him or her according to the terms of what was agreed upon. Especially if we have the money set aside to do that very thing.

After the job is finished and once the effort has been put forth to complete a task *IS NOT* the time to renegotiate terms of compensation. Pay what you owe. Don't nick-pick a job trying to get out of paying what was agreed upon.

Also, part of the generosity package is that we have some grace around the final results of the project. It might be that the results of that job are fantastic and awesome, we write the check, and its done and dusted. A simple deal and everyone is happy!

Then there are times when maybe the project didn't turn out so hot. It might be time for some straight talk about the terms and expectations and how some things might be corrected, but we still have some obligation for manpower and materials that have been used and sourced in the deal. I think the warning is not to allow disappointment or our passion about the outcome, determine your heart in how you are going to react in a less than favorable situation.

If we are going to err, will we err on the side of grace and generosity; or will the person we're dealing with walk away mumbling: *"What a frikk'n hard ass!"* You can resolve the deal without having to be a tyrant!

I know we hear often, *"If you don't demand satisfaction, people will walk all over you!"* This is a real likelihood, but I think the Lord was dialed into these realities:

"But I say to you who hear, love your enemies, do good to those who hate you, bless those who curse you, pray for those who mistreat you. Whoever hits you on the cheek, offer him the other also; and whoever takes away your coat, do not withhold your shirt from him either. Give to everyone who asks of you, and whoever takes away what is yours, do not demand it back" (Luke 6:27-30, NASB).

You want to talk about hard! Wow! But, He is confirming this whole idea of us being the graceful weight on the seesaw!

We go Wall Street sometimes when our money is involved and we start pushing and shoving and carelessly become demanding and demeaning towards people, which is the normal way that business is handled out there. Deals go sour, but that isn't a viable excuse for us to loose our mind and witness.

Wisdom is encouraging us to go beyond and do more than what is expected. To handle the difficult situations gracefully; and the normal procedures with integrity and uprightness!

All without necessarily trying to put another soul notch on your belt! It is a real blessing for people and for you when grace lands heavy. People rarely expect it!

In The Pages

Have you ever been paid properly for a job that you know you didn't do completely as the terms dictated? Why do you think you were paid in that situation? What lessons did you learn?

The Center of Our Center

April 4
Proverbs 4

"My son, give attention to my words; incline your ear to my sayings. Do not let them depart from your sight; keep them in the midst of your heart. For they are life to those who find them and health to all their body." Proverbs 4:20-22, NASB

"But have nothing to do with worldly fables fit only for old women. On the other hand, discipline yourself for the purpose of godliness; for bodily discipline is only of little profit, but godliness is profitable for all things, since it holds promise for the present life and also for the life to come." 1 Timothy 4:7-8, NASB

I love Solomon's recognition of the obvious connection between the stuff that is going on in our heart and the overall health of our natural bodies. It is shocking really, that more often than not; we (including most Christians) rarely see the correlation!

Wikipedia reports that Americans are the biggest spenders on healthcare in the world. I'm sure that is not much of a surprise. In 2009, we spent $2.5 trillion on healthcare. That averages out to $8,047 per person, on medical, hospital and pharmaceutical costs.

An article in the May 2008 edition of Time magazine reported that each year, the economic cost of untreated mental illness is staggering — over $100 billion on untreated mental health disorders and $400 billion on addiction disorders.

According to that same article, serious mental illnesses, which afflict about six percent of American adults, cost our society $193.2 billion in lost earnings per year. It would seem prudent for us to at least ask the question:

"Is any of this physical stuff messing with us spiritually generated?"

You would think we would at least ask the question... right? {Sigh} **Wrong**. We do NOT seem to be able to connect the dots.

Solomon is asking his children to store the wisdom he has passed on to them, deep inside, *"in the midst,"* in the bi-sections, the centers of their inner-man (their wills, their feelings, their intellects - the centers of their whole lives).

So, if he were to give them an anatomy lesson, Solomon would say,

"The heart is your center for life. Inside of your heart, in the middle of your heart, is a septum. That is where I want you to store wisdom. In the center of your center, keep these truths to live by!"

"Why Daddy... why do I put wisdom there?"

"Because your center has everything to do with how you experience and live your life. Your center has more to do with your actual health than you'll ever be able to articulate. Don't cut corners here! Keep wisdom at the center of your center and the rest of your body will align itself accordingly."

In looking at the numbers, we don't have much to lose. It might be that we need to give serious consideration to what the ancient voice of Wisdom is telling us. This is an understanding that appears to be broken. Only we can fix it.

In The Pages

What other truths rocked you in today's passages? Do you ever consider your spiritual condition when your body ails? What is your first reaction when you feel bad: to self-medicate or to pray?

Pond Scum

April 5
Proverbs 5

"Or you will give your vigor to others and your years to the cruel one." Proverbs 5:9, NASB

"Like a broken record." There is a good chance many of you have no idea what it sounds like to have a scratched vinyl record looping the same words over and over until you have to manually remove the arm and needle of the player. The iPod generation is clueless about such things.

Whether you have common knowledge or not, Proverbs has some serious grooves that loop certain messages over and over. The pain and hazards of illicit sexual conduct is a common download by Solomon.

He loved his children and was continually driving home the notion, *"It's just not worth it! Drink water from your own well. Eat your own fruit. Enjoy the gourmet meal and put away the junk food!"*

In today's text, Solomon uses very vivid language to help make his point. To sleep around, fool around, get around, or lay it down, was to *give* away *"your vigor and your years to the cruel one".* Whatever that means, it definitely suggests this is wasteful, reckless and overall poor stewardship of one's God-given life resources and vitality.

"Vigor" is an interesting word. The Hebrew word is **hôwd** (pronounced *hode*), and it means, *"grandeur or imposing form."* Several different translations use the word "honor" instead (KJV, NKJV, RSV). It can mean that, but I don't think we would naturally equate "honor" with the rest of the ideas attached to "vigor," such as, *beauty, excellence, comeliness, glory and majesty.*

I sense that *"vigor"* is the right word simply because there is more at stake than your good reputation. To diminish yourself in this kind of arena sucks the very life out of you.

As if that isn't destructive enough, I can pretty much assure you that the accuser (the devil) will condemn and pour out more than enough torment to erode your peace. Sleep will elude you. Stress will find you. Paranoia will torment and steal your internal and natural rhythm.

Every time you attempt to move in faith or righteous intent, you'll hear the voice of the adversary tell you that no matter what you do for God, it will never wash away the stains of your failure. The devil usually uses some portion of truth against us. We're too smart to buy a total fabrication.

It would be an error to believe that you cannot be forgiven. Forgiveness is readily available to everyone, but you have to get that forgiveness from the Lord, and whoever else was wounded by your actions.

You can't appease the guilt by doing good works. You'll be so sidetracked from the condemnation and complications of your choices that it will be hard to decipher who is friend, and who is foe.

In short, you'll give away the very best you have to offer – yourself. Do yourself (and whoever else might be a potential candidate for such shenanigans) a favor:

FISH IN YOUR OWN POND

If you don't have a pond, wait for one!

Sexual roulette is a dangerous game played with a bullet in every chamber. It's a cruel game that takes away the best you have to give.

In The Pages

Why do you think this message is mostly ignored in our culture? What damage have you seen done by premarital sex or adulterous activity?

Yes and No

April 6
Proverbs 6

"A scoundrel and villain, who goes about with a corrupt mouth, who winks with his eye, signals with his feet and motions with his fingers, who plots evil with deceit in his heart— he always stirs up dissension." Proverbs 6:12-14, NIV

"Nor shall you make an oath by your head, for you cannot make one hair white or black. But let your statement be, 'Yes, yes' or 'No, no'; anything beyond these is of evil." Matthew 5:36-37, NASB

The problem starts with deceit in the heart. There isn't any way to soften this. The deceitful heart is a heart full of fraud and *evil plotting*.

Jesus didn't see that it was necessary to make big proclamations of promise in order to assure someone of your intentions or integrity. Let your *"yes"* be a yes, and also let your *"no"* mean no. Deal straight with people without having to make guarantees that either you can't keep, or do not intend to keep.

We all appreciate simple trust, real truth and honesty. We all do! But when I walk through the mall and the hawkers at the kiosk reach for me, promising to save me "big money," I turn a deaf ear. They are NOT interested in saving me big money! NO way! They want me to buy their products. The more they lean, the less inclined I am to grab my wallet.

It's not all crooked, but sometimes it feels that way. I like a store that allows me to shop without pressure. When I ask a question, they respond with information, but no pressure. That's how I like to buy stuff.

I have mixed emotions about how I used to do some stuff. While attending seminary, I took a course on how to do door-to-door evangelism. We set goals and quotas on the number of visits and personal contacts we should have.

I was coached on all kinds of things—good things I guess—but it was all about the presentation. You had to know how to deal with the objections, with the interruptions and cold receptions.

I knew then, as I know now, that Jesus is a difference maker. My evangelical roots are fairly firm in that belief. So, I was young, eager, excited, driven and religiously zealous.

But honestly, I wish I had been much more interested in the people I was trying to convert. Sadly, too many times, I was no different from the guy at the mall, making my pitch, working my deal, trying to get them to do what I wanted them to do.

Lots of people prayed the prayer I wanted them to pray, but I don't have a clue who they really were, where they are now or if any of the mud I was slinging even stuck to the walls.

God knows and that is where I get my comfort, but I could have done it differently. Fortunately, HIS heart was always right. That part I can guarantee!

I still think people need to know what Jesus did for them. I still believe that people need to meet the real Father in God. I still have the conviction that people need the filling of the Holy Spirit, but I try to truly convey HIS heart with the smiles and love I give them.

I want to hear their stories. I want to earn their trust through relationship, without having to lay down the "medicine show" for my own benefit.

As my salesman father says, *"The key is helping people who are ready to buy! People want to trust and buy from a friend. We facilitate what they want to do... not what we want them to do."*

I think this could also apply to our Jesus. The real Jesus is an easy to market.

In The Pages

Do you know how to share your faith with another person when they ask questions? How did you enter into your relationship with God?

Honestly, I don't handle people in these terms anymore. I'm convinced that the love of God for his children overwhelms how we respond to him. "IT WAS FOR FREEDOM THAT CHRIST HAS SET US FREE." I'm almost

certain that it includes our religious beliefs, expressions, and zeal. We are righteous because of what God did for us... not how we perform. —MDP 2018

Cunning Heart

April 7
Proverbs 7

"And behold, a woman comes to meet him, dressed as a harlot and cunning of heart." Proverbs 7:10, NASB

A long time ago (I love grand stories that begin this way, although this story isn't so grand), a friend of mine used to be a pimp.[1] He bought, sold, abused, rented and traded women. Their bodies were his commodities. Prostitution was the business.

He has since given his life over to the Lord and married one of the women who used to work for him. He has a beautiful family now and a busy ministry. Many things have changed since "a long time ago."

One day, while sharing a meal together, I quizzed his wife a bit to find out what her world had been like. I had heard crazy stories that seemed only possible in the movies. I asked her, *"Sister C, what kind of money did your clientele pay for your services?"*

This beautiful woman with the radiant smile gave me that "nosey boy wants information" look. She is a high-energy, Type A personality, still fairly young, with an edgy attitude, but she went easy on me:

Pastor Mike, our clientele were upscale. We moved with politicians, lawyers, preachers, movers-n-shakers, the privileged, the white collar and the money crowd. My job was to find out how much money you had. I assessed everything; your watch, your clothes, even your car... all of it. It was a game. Whatever you had, that was what I cost. If you had $300, that was what I cost. If you had $3,000, that was what I cost. A client wanted what I had to offer. I wanted what I wanted and that was total control of what they had."

I was fairly shocked. I'm not even sure what I thought I was going to hear, but I should have known. It was all about the *"cunning heart"*.

I don't think I remember reading anything in the Gospels where Jesus was demeaning or condemning to a prostitute or an adulterer.

He was always about undoing our shame (John 8:11), promoting self-awareness, and encouraging us to change.

Friar Richard Rohr calls this the *"Gift of Guilt."* This is when we are stimulated to own our character defects. We stop denial, we give up rationalization and we own what we need to own.

Jesus does this while removing the shame (which is our fear of man's opinion), loss of respect, and the suspicion of being hated or absolutely rejected.

Make no mistake, a *"cunning heart"* can manifest in more than just the Midnight Lady. It is something that every one of us has to wrestle down. Owning our faults, our weakness, our sins and our lack of faith makes us targets for accusation and judgment.

But the Lord moves towards us, not away from us. He knows us better than we know ourselves. He doesn't blush in religious piety when you tell Him your story.

He can take the raw truth when you are ready to be real about the details. Remember, it is the truth that sets us free (John 8:32). It is in the light that we can see.

It is His love that holds us until we can purge all the deceit. *Blessed is the man whose sin the Lord does not count against him and in whose spirit is no deceit"* (Psalms 32:2, NIV).

Yes and Amen!

In The Pages

What is the primary lesson of today's Proverb? How does the Holy Spirit apply and settle these truths in your heart?

Straight and Forward

April 8
Proverbs 8

"They are all straightforward to him who understands, and right to those who find knowledge." Proverbs 8:9, NASB

*"**But when Cephas came to Antioch, I opposed him to his face**, because he stood condemned. For prior to the coming of certain men from James, he used to eat with the Gentiles; but when they came, he began to withdraw and hold himself aloof, fearing the party of the circumcision. The rest of the Jews **joined him in hypocrisy**; with the result that even **Barnabas was carried away by their hypocrisy. But when I saw that they were not straightforward about the truth of the gospel, I said to Cephas in the presence of all,** 'If you, being a Jew, live like the Gentiles and not like the Jews, how is it that you compel the Gentiles to live like Jews? We are Jews by nature and not sinners from among the Gentiles; nevertheless knowing that a man is not justified by the works of the Law but through faith in Christ Jesus, even we have believed in Christ Jesus, so that we may be justified by faith in Christ and not by the works of the Law; since by the works of the Law no flesh will be justified. But if, while seeking to be justified in Christ, we ourselves have also been found sinners, is Christ then a minister of sin? May it never be! For if I rebuild what I have once destroyed, I prove myself to be a transgressor. For through the Law I died to the Law, so that I might live to God. I have been crucified with Christ; and it is no longer I who live, but Christ lives in me; and the life, which I now live in the flesh I live by faith in the Son of God, who loved me and gave Himself up for me. I do not nullify the grace of God, for if righteousness comes through the Law, then Christ died needlessly.' "* Galatians 2:11-21, NASB

The basic premise in today's Proverb is that Lady Wisdom tells it like it really is. Even if it requires her to "front you out," she will not spare your feelings.

Truth is truth, and she offers the real deal without apology. The words of wisdom are *"straightforward,"* equitable, plain, upright, blunt and without spin. We're not used to that.

Most everything in our world (politics, religion, talk radio, sports) is served to us through our evening newscasters, who break down and analyze the facts for us (through their superior intellect and warm understanding hearts, no doubt) so the rest of us can be up to speed. Wisdom doesn't do all of that. It takes raw truth and serves it just that way—RAW. It's up to us to analyze and break it down.

He was "the" Peter, for Heaven's sake! Not just "Peter the fisherman," but the guy Jesus pointed at and said, *"You're da man! The rock upon which I'll build my church"* (Matthew 16:18).

With the precision of a crafty prosecuting attorney, the sham was over. With *straightforward* audacity, Peter stood condemned, along with Barnabas, by the laser-edged tongue of Paul. Read that Galatians passage again. Wow! What a rebuke!

But with so much at stake, it had to happen. There needed to be some clarity. Peter was the one who got the initial download about the Gentiles in the first place, but "religious devils" wanted to keep the Old Law alive by ritual.

It was all that religious pressure that made them act the way they did, despite what they knew to be truth! Can we say AMEN for Paul's willingness to call out and front out his friends in plain, upright, blunt truth? Now that is wisdom!

In The Pages

My favorite verse in today's devo is Galatians 2:16 *"Nevertheless knowing that a man is not justified by the works of the Law but through faith in Christ Jesus, even we have believed in Christ Jesus, so that we may be justified by faith in Christ and not by the works of the Law; since by the works of the Law no flesh will be justified"* (NASB). Which is yours? Why?

Screech Owls

April 9
Proverbs 9

"Do not correct a scoffer, lest he hate you; rebuke a wise man and he will love you." Proverbs 9:8, NIV

"'Behold, you scoffers, and marvel, and perish; for I am accomplishing a work in your days, a work which you will never believe, though someone should describe it to you.' *As Paul and Barnabas were going out, the people kept begging that these things might be spoken to them the next Sabbath. Now when the meeting of the synagogue had broken up, many of the Jews and of the God-fearing proselytes followed Paul and Barnabas, who, speaking to them, were urging them to continue in the grace of God." Acts 13:41-43, NASB*

The Hebrew word for *"scoffer"* is **lîylîyth** (pronounced *lee-leeth'*), and it means, *"screech owl."*

Many years ago, I had a bad attitude towards ducks. I hunted them really hard. In the worst of conditions (rain, sleet, muck, frozen waters—the worse it was, the better I liked it), I would stand for countless hours in waders and camo just to knock those skilled kamikazes out of the sky.

One morning, hours before daylight, I was lugging a large sack of decoys through quiet woods. About the time my flashlight went dead, a very large screech owl flew within inches over my head, screaming some high-pitched noise (I may have pee'd myself just a little bit).

It came out of nowhere and without warning. I was undone for about 10 minutes. That sound was absolutely horrific and the entire incident left a lasting memory!

Wisdom correctly asserts that it is a waste of time to attempt to reason with someone who, by nature or choice, isn't willing to listen. The Apostles knew very well that there would always be some religious spirit hanging around to automatically challenge anything that didn't sound like tradition.

Before any attempt would be made to absorb the possibility of a new truth, *scoffers* would go "offensive" with shrill rhetoric in an attempt to shut them down. Paul was on his first missionary journey when he quoted this Habakkuk passage (found in Acts 13:41).

Trying to bring the new revelation to people who were not really willing to listen was tiresome and grating. Some of Paul's efforts are likened to trying to talk to children who put their fingers in their ears, chanting, *"lah lah lah"* as loud as they could!

Old school Jews wanted nothing to do with his insight and teachings about the Christ. He was called to help both Jew and Gentile to see, but the most obstinate pushback came from Jewish *scoffers*.

When people aren't listening and are instead running interference, it's time to stop talking. Arguing is actually counter-productive.

Jesus was very familiar with *scoffers* and this is what he offered, *"Do not give what is holy to dogs, and do not throw your pearls before swine, or they will trample them under their feet, and turn and tear you to pieces"* (Matthew 7:6, NASB). I think that was Lady Wisdom's exact point.

In The Pages

Have you ever argued a religious point with someone who did not want to listen? How did it make you feel afterwards? Did the discussion end on the same topic in which it began?

These days I can't imagine a reason to be involved in a religious argument with another person. If I can't persuade them with loving actions... surely my beating them with bible quotes and my brand of theology is pointless! Love

is what breaks yokes. Certainly not my opinions and certitudes. —MDP 2018

Play Ball!

April 10
Proverbs 10

"The blessing of the Lord, it maketh rich, and he addeth no sorrow with it. It is as sport to a fool to do mischief: but a man of understanding hath wisdom." Proverbs 10:22-23, KJV

For baseball fans, the long wait of winter is over. Baseball is finally here! If this past off-season was anything like the last 45 years of history since I've been paying attention, there was probably a player trade or a contract deal offered that has set a new standard for what MLB owners are willing to pay their star players. It is astounding how much professional athletes get paid to play the game of baseball.

As a result, ticket prices continue to climb and the concessions are insanely expensive, yet we keep filling the seats (unless your team absolutely sucks) because we Americans have a long-standing love affair with the game of baseball.

I guess we deserve what we tolerate.

That being said, as long as everything is on the up and up, it's all-good! But when we read in the headlines that somebody cheated, someone cut a corner or not everyone played fairly, it feels… well, quite frankly, sad.

The game is so steeped in the tradition of stats and records that any infidelity whatsoever really throws a wrench in the gearbox. Historically, players, coaches, owners and even umpires who have been caught cheating in one way or another have been banned from the game all together. It won't be long until someone gets banned for PEDs. It's bound to happen soon!

It seems utterly ridiculous that a business/game that is so lucrative in all its benefits would be afflicted by such nonsense. Wisdom would simply advise: work hard, play fair and enjoy the money that you rightfully earned! But activity contrary to those standards brings a shame and torment that is filled with all kinds of hurt and sorrow.

One of the commentators I regularly consult suggests that today's Proverb is a condensed thought from Solomon on a different passage he also shared in Psalms 127:1-2:

"Unless the Lord builds the house, they labor in vain who build it; unless the Lord guards the city, the watchman keeps awake in vain. It is vain for you to rise up early, to retire late, to eat the bread of painful labors; for He gives to His beloved even in his sleep" (NASB).

The summary is simple:

The Lord is the source of all just blessing, and that includes riches!

To tamper with and acquire unjustly is to bring a great hurt upon yourself and those associated with your methods.

One more reminder from the text: *"But you shall remember the Lord your God, for it is He who is giving you power to make wealth"* (Deuteronomy 8:18, NASB).

Stewarding such blessing is vastly important. We could all probably pay a little more attention to these things regardless of the sizes of our paychecks!

In The Pages

Please read Hosea 2:1-13 (remember that the prophet is giving voice to God's insight of Israel's ways). Journal your thoughts concerning this verbiage found in verse 8. Who was behind the blessings? How does this relate to today?

Reciprocal

April 11
Proverbs 11

"The merciful man does himself good, but the cruel man does himself harm."
Proverbs 11:17, NASB

"But when the Son of Man comes in His glory, and all the angels with Him, then He will sit on His glorious throne. All the nations will be gathered before Him; and He will separate them from one another, as the shepherd separates the sheep from the goats; and He will put the sheep on His right, and the goats

on the left. Then the King will say to those on His right, 'Come, you who are blessed of My Father, inherit the kingdom prepared for you from the foundation of the world. 'For I was hungry, and you gave Me something to eat; I was thirsty, and you gave Me something to drink; I was a stranger, and you invited Me in; naked, and you clothed Me; I was sick, and you visited Me; I was in prison, and you came to Me.' Then the righteous will answer Him, 'Lord, when did we see You hungry, and feed You, or thirsty, and give You something to drink? And when did we see You a stranger, and invite You in, or naked, and clothe You? When did we see You sick, or in prison, and come to You?' The King will answer and say to them, **'Truly I say to you, to the extent that you did it to one of these brothers of Mine, even the least of them, you did it to Me.'** *Then He will also say to those on His left, 'Depart from Me, accursed ones, into the eternal fire which has been prepared for the devil and his angels; for I was hungry, and you gave Me nothing to eat; I was thirsty, and you gave Me nothing to drink; I was a stranger, and you did not invite Me in; naked, and you did not clothe Me; sick, and in prison, and you did not visit Me.' Then they themselves also will answer, 'Lord, when did we see You hungry, or thirsty, or a stranger, or naked, or sick, or in prison, and did not take care of You?' Then He will answer them, 'Truly I say to you, to the extent that you did not do it to one of the least of these, you did not do it to Me.' These will go away into eternal punishment, but the righteous into eternal life."* Matthew 25:31-46, NASB

Can we just forget about who's in and who's out and all that eschatological thought for a moment and just focus on the simple message that Jesus equates our loving on the lost and hurting of this world as loving on Him?

We can never really reciprocate what He has done for us, other than to love Him and love those whom He loves. Without stirring a theological dust storm, just see the fact that He notices.

Wisdom instructs clearly that acts of mercy pay back dividends of mercy. Jesus confirms it: *"Blessed are the merciful, for they shall receive mercy"* (Matthew 5:7, NASB).

Without a doubt, it is a happier way to live. A fuller existence that is soaked in a Kingdom marinade. There isn't any reason to even debate this notion. This is the DNA of the followers of Jesus. We are to be instruments of mercy, tools in His hands, the touch that the broken can trust.

The prophet says it so clearly, *"Assyria will not save us, we will not ride on horses; nor will we say again, 'Our god,' to the work of our hands; for in You the orphan finds mercy"* (Hosea 14:3, NASB).

In The Pages

Have you ever had the thought, "I am mercy?" What would have to change in your life paradigm for that to be truth? What would have to alter in your value system for mercy to flow naturally from you?

Richard Rohr O.F.M. wisely states, "Our image of God creates us." How do you really view God? Take an honest look at yourself. Are you living proof of God's mercy, grace, and love? Are you patient, kind, and inclusive in your way with mankind? God is LOVE. Is that the fragrance of your life? —MDP 2018

Better Than a Kick in the Butt

April 12
Proverbs 12

"Better is he who is lightly esteemed and has a servant than he who honors himself and lacks bread." Proverbs 12:9, NASB

I'm always blown away by the amount of data smart people are able to compile about stuff in the Bible. It's incredible really.

The Bible Knowledge Commentary reports that today's verse is the first of 19 verses in Proverbs that use the 'better… than' formula" (12:9; 15:16-17; 16:8, 16, 19, 32; 17:1, 12; 19:1, 22; 21:9, 19; 22:1; 25:7, 24; 27:5, 10; 28:6). We'll dig in there deeper later, but I hear the formula used all the time. It's usually a concession we make for whatever circumstance we're dealing with.

As a kid, I'd wrinkle my nose at some vegetable I didn't like (because I had never tried it) and I'd hear about "Starvin' Marvin" in Africa. It was my mom's way of reminding me whatever we were eating was better than nothing! It was hard to complain when the images of Marvin were in the room.

My personal favorite is, *"Well, that's better than a kick in the butt!"* I have no idea where I picked that up and I'm not too sure it offers Patti much consolation when she tells me she's having a bad hair day. She's just learned over the years that it's better to let it end there than to comment. Any remark from her just opens the door for more of my profound wisdom. She's a quick learner.

The heart of today's verse touches us again about pretense. It's just better to be real about our lives and situations.

I've often thought that, of all places, Church should be the place that is without pretense. When I think about this for too long I can get pretty wound up over it all. Recently, I read from Paul's own words about how he had settled himself with some things he couldn't control. It's an amazing insight!

"Now I want you to know, brethren, that my circumstances have turned out for the greater progress of the gospel, so that my imprisonment in the cause of Christ has become well known throughout the whole praetorian guard and to everyone else, and that most of the brethren, trusting in the Lord because of my imprisonment, have far more courage to speak the word of God without fear. Some, to be sure, are preaching Christ even from envy and strife, but some also from good will; the latter do it out of love, knowing that I am appointed for the defense of the gospel; the former proclaim Christ out of selfish ambition rather than from pure motives, thinking to cause me distress in my imprisonment" (Philippians 1:12-17, NASB).

So here we have the Apostle in chains, out of sight, but not off of God's radar. Stuff looked a little crappy out there, and I would imagine it was difficult to watch the pretenders take advantage of his predicament. Would it be better for it to have been different?

In a perfect world, the short answer would be: **PROBABLY**.

But it's not a perfect world and stuff rarely goes as we imagine or plan it. I'm sure this wasn't "Plan A" in Paul's mind, but he saw again for himself that God was at work, even though his personal circumstances sucked. He amazingly adds, *"What then? Only that in every way, whether in pretense or in truth, Christ is proclaimed; and in this I rejoice. Yes, and I will rejoice"* (Philippians 1:18, NASB).

Paul has looked it over and decided; if *"Christ is proclaimed"* is the bottom-line… that's much better than a kick in his butt!

In The Pages

What other insight did you get out of this Philippians passage? How much patience do you have with those more or less zealous about their faith in Christ? How worried did Paul seem to you?

Walking the Walk

April 13
Proverbs 13

"He who walks with the wise grows wise, but a companion of fools suffers harm." Proverbs 13:20, NIV

"He has told you, O man, what is good; and what does the Lord require of you but to do justice, to love kindness, and to walk humbly with your God?" Micah 6:8, NASB

The prophet Micah is referring to Deuteronomy 30:15-16:

"See, I have set before you today life and prosperity, and death and adversity; in that I command you today to love the Lord your God, to walk in His ways and to keep His commandments and His statutes and His judgments, that you may live and multiply, and that the Lord your God may bless you in the land where you are entering to possess it." (NASB)

This whole idea of "walking with" someone has everything to do with our development. If you walk with an angry person, be prepared to have to fight sometimes. If you walk with a greedy person, be prepared to be a victim of their greed. If you walk with a controller, don't be surprised when you find yourself being controlled.

In contrast, walking with people who love, *really* love, unconditionally, can wreck your life for the good! Healthy folk who are full of grace slosh grace everywhere they go. If you walk with them, you're bound to get some of that on you also! And as Solomon suggests, seeking out and walking with people who are full of wisdom releases that same spirit into our mind, heart, and ultimately our character.

To me, the real tragedy in the Garden wasn't that Adam and Eve got kicked out, but that they lost the unbridled privilege to walk openly **with** the Lord. The ease of communion, the thoughtful consideration of that paradise, was gone forever.

Now it seems we have to make the constant choice to push into fellowship with the Lord. He's not avoiding us, but He's actually honoring our freedom to choose in or out of the relationship. It's the only way He knows that we want in! Thus, we get this message from the Lord to walk in His ways, to keep and follow the paths that He promises to bless.

The very heart of *discipleship* is relationship—walking together in real-time communion. Too many of us have reduced the process to assignments and commissions of duty.

Any secular or religious organization can give you assignments and tasks... BUT that doesn't mean discipleship is happening.

The Lord didn't tell the disciples to *"follow me,"* and then immediately give them a list of things to do or throw them at a problem He needed them to fix. For three years they had constant access to Jesus' life... his thoughts... his way of handling people.

They didn't get sent out until they were ready. His departure didn't happen until it was time. Finger math would suggest they were in his proximity for about 17,500 waking hours. That is a staggering thought!

The process of *"walking with"* does work, and we can become like Whom we walk with IF we are willing to put in the time to develop the relationship.

In The Pages

How would you define discipleship? Is your definition different from the one you were raised with?

Gumdrops and Cupcakes

April 14
Proverbs 14

"Leave the presence of a fool, or you will not discern words of knowledge. The wisdom of the sensible is to understand his way, but the foolishness of fools is deceit. Fools mock at sin, but among the upright there is good will." Proverbs 14:7-9, NASB

I want to continue on with yesterday's thoughts about choosing well when it comes to whom we *walk with* in our lives. Today's verse again confirms to us that there can be negative implications to walking with people who don't have the same value systems as we do. Solomon fronts out the *fool*, and we become just like him if we are not willing to part ways.

The wisdom of the King points out three drawbacks to walking with a fool.

First, **you risk your own loss of discernment.**

Second, **you'll find yourself in swirls of deceit and confusion that the fool has created for those around him.**

Third, **you'll be guilty by association when the fool makes fun of the destruction he has created by his own stupidity and sin.**

I honestly believe that those who hung around Jesus got the ripest fruits of the Spirit.

"But the fruit of the Spirit is love, joy, peace, patience, kindness, goodness, faithfulness, gentleness, self-control" (Galatians 5:22-23, NASB).

He was satiated with all of those qualities. It wasn't just how He acted... it was who He was.

The disciples benefited greatly under His authority and life. They didn't always manifest those gifts all of the time (they were men, not deity), but they were vastly influenced by His words and life.

But if you think He was all gumdrops and cupcakes, you might need to adjust your thinking. Jesus had strong warnings to his followers about whom they followed and what they submitted themselves to.

Exhibit A - *"The scribes and the Pharisees have seated themselves in the chair of Moses; therefore all that they tell you, do and observe, but do not do according to their deeds; for they say things and do not do them"* (Matthew 23:2-3, NASB).

For the rest of that chapter Jesus pretty much rips the Pharisees a new butt hole. Peterson (MSG) titles that chapter (Matthew 23) ***"The Religious Fashion Show."*** They deserved what they got.

Again, the problem was that Jesus didn't want his sheep following those kinds of leaders. There was such a contradiction in what they were saying, compared to how they were actually living, that it kept a chaotic fire-storm constantly stirred over the people.

Our Master took serious offense to the Pharisees' ways and strongly warned people not to be swayed by all their smoke and mirrors.

Today, we do 10-15 hours of Bible Study, a Skype call here, a conference call there, and we call it *discipleship*. It can include these things, but it takes years and years to develop people spiritually. It is grueling work, sometimes monotonous, often mundane, mostly unappreciated and extremely time consuming!

After three years of public ministry, I'm fairly certain that Jesus and his tribe of 12 were all near exhaustion! But the bonds they had, what He had been put into them, what forged them together, had been worth every minute!

Their walk long after His departure still feeds the masses! They made a good choice in following Him.

In The Pages

Do you see the cost of those who pour out in discipleship? How do you best honor those who have fed you? Could it be that it's now time to feed others?

Abyss

April 15
Proverbs 15

"Hell and Destruction are before the Lord; so how much more the hearts of the sons of men." Proverbs 15:11, NKJV

"Sheol and Abaddon lie open before the Lord, how much more the hearts of men!" Proverbs 15:11, NASB

Oscar: "Ok, Mr. Truman, let's say that we actually do land on this. What's it gonna be like up there?"

Truman: "200 degrees in the sunlight, minus 200 in the shade, canyons of razor sharp rock, unpredictable gravitational conditions, unexpected eruptions, things like that."

Oscar: "Okay, so the scariest environment imaginable. Thanks. That's all you gotta say, scariest environment imaginable." From the movie *Armageddon*

Other than the general consensus that *"Hell and Destruction"* are bad, there isn't much talk about what it all means. Is it real? Is it real today? How the heck does it affect all of us? Good questions.

I don't think Solomon was necessarily agitating some theological turd-storm for us here. The understanding at the time was simple: NOT MUCH. But as traditional orthodoxy developed, the common understanding recognized *Sheol* (*Hell*) and *Abaddon* (*Destruction*) as references to the geographical dwelling of the dead found in the depths of the earth.

It's kind of a sore subject right now by the way people are acting about it, but I'm fairly convinced that *Hell* might be—probably is—a "place" that really does exist. But ultimately, I see *Hell* manifested on earth on a regular basis by people who confess that their final destination is already secured in Heaven, which is quite disturbing paradox.

I've got way too much evangelical teaching in me to just blow off any of the possibilities. Besides, as I've already indicated, I see evidence of *Hell* all the time.

Blatant legalism, hate, religious devils, self-seeking, jealousy, selfish-ambition, self-promotion, self-absorption and the continued exploitation of humanity by other humans—all convince me that the work of *Hell*, the devil, demons and any other byproduct of *Destruction* are fully alive, organized and active all over the earth! Oh yeah, even here in the good ole U.S. of A.

But to tell you the truth, when I saw today's Proverb, I didn't have any of what I just wrote on my heart. What I had in my spirit was an overwhelming thankfulness that our God—the Blessed Trinity—really knows us and sees us deeply!

So, IF those places are legit and even *Hell* and *Destruction* are before the Lord and He sees all of it clearly, then all of our hurts and disappointments, our wounds and aches, are also well within His range of view.

He sees everything!

Our beloved David wrote, *"Search me, O God, and know my heart; try me and know my anxious thoughts; and see if there be any hurtful way in me, and lead me in the everlasting way"* (Psalms 139:23-24, NASB). But God already had! He already knew the depths of David's heart! In that regard, nothing has changed. He sees.

In The Pages

So when you read today's Proverbs, what part struck you first? Are you fascinated with afterlife? What are your conclusions about such things? How do they help you live in the full expression of the Kingdom today?

Nasty Burp

April 16
Proverbs 16

"Before destruction is pride, and before stumbling—a haughty spirit. Better is humility of spirit with the poor, than to apportion spoil with the proud." Proverbs 16:18-19, YLT

It doesn't appear that King Solomon is allowing any wiggle room here for exceptions, special cases or anomalies. There is no soft net of grace for this particular bad boy. He's pretty confident that the entailment of pride is destruction, and the ramification for a haughty spirit is stumbling. This is confirmed several different places in Proverbs. For example:

"When pride comes, then comes dishonor, but with the humble is wisdom" (Proverbs 11:2, NASB)

AND

"Before destruction the heart of man is haughty, but humility goes before honor" (Proverbs 18:12, NASB)

Say what you will, but it's not good! Part of the problem here is that we usually relegate *pride* to behavioral traits. We pigeonhole it; we assume that if people would simply change their behavior, it would be the end of the story. But *pride* is a demonic spirit that can operate in and through people, families, organizations, governments—just about anything, especially the church.

It influences thought and attitudes of well-being. It usually provides the justification needed to confirm this errant behavior. So, there is much more involved than simply fixing stuff on the *outside*. Things have to shift on the *inside* in order to kill *pride*.

There is a passage of scripture in the Gospel of Mark that reveals Jesus' insight concerning our capacity for doing evil. Check this out:

"After He called the crowd to Him again, He began saying to them, "Listen to Me, all of you, and understand: there is nothing outside the man which can defile him if it goes into him; but the things which proceed out of the man are what defile the man. ["If anyone has ears to hear, let him hear."] When he had left the crowd and entered the house, His disciples questioned Him about the parable. And He *said to them, "Are you so lacking in understanding also? Do you not understand that whatever goes into the man from outside cannot defile him, because it does not go into his heart, but into his stomach, and is

eliminated?" (Thus He declared all foods clean.) And He was saying, "That which proceeds out of the man, that is what defiles the man. For from within, out of the heart of men, proceed the **evil thoughts**, **fornications**, **thefts**, **murders**, **adulteries**, **deeds of coveting** *and* **wickedness**, *as well as* **deceit, sensuality, envy, slander, pride** *and* **foolishness**. *All these evil things proceed from within and defile the man"* Mark 7:14-23, (NASB).

I actually love this passage because He responds to all those nervous Christians who want to know whether or not certain behaviors are acceptable—especially those who fear that a sip of wine (external), or tobacco (external), or certain kinds of foods (external), might trigger the disapproval of God.

Jesus was always focused on what His father was focused on, which was the heart of man. It's *inside* of us that all the problems reside. So Jesus addresses his concerns (here's the list one more time in case you weren't paying attention): evil thoughts, fornications, thefts, murders, adulteries, deeds of coveting and wickedness, as well as deceit, sensuality, envy, slander, *pride* and foolishness. Yeah, it can get pretty ugly in there (*internal*), and the Pharisees' infatuation with the *externals* was simple stupidity compared to this lovely list of what actually defiles us.

Right there, Jesus tells us that *pride* is a "nasty burp" of mankind. Don't think for a moment that *pride* goes unnoticed in the spirit realm. Every demon in hell welcomes any opportunity to connect with the cause.

Pride loves religious activity. *Pride* and selfish ambition are kissing cousins. *Pride* and bigotry, *pride* and elitism, *pride* and genocide, are almost inseparable.

Solomon was definitely laying down some serious truth here. The quickest path to destruction is through our involvement with *pride*. The bigger issue is that it is *IN* us.

In The Pages

Have you ever been told you were prideful? How did you respond to that? Is pride in your family lineage? How does it manifest? Do you have pride?

Good Medicine

April 17
Proverbs 17

"A joyful heart is good medicine, but a broken spirit dries up the bones." Proverbs 17:22, NASB

This is a sheer act of my will today (2012). I'm sick. Frik! It's one of those viral jobs where your temperature can be 98.1 or 101.1, depending on when you check it. I throw up from coughing. It sounds like a full-on exorcism when I'm really cranking.

When I was a kid, I had what they call "Whooping Cough." I developed the technique for loosening the slime in my bronchia by coughing. As I said, the sounds of my "episodes" are infamous within my family. My children still pee a little when I start hacking.

I can remember the early morning tents and hot showers that my parents gave me, hoping the steam would give me some relief. So today, I *feel* sucky, *sound* sucky, and I've been *in* bed more than I've been *out of* bed. I'm pretty much pitiful.

If Patti squirts me with Lysol one more time, I am going to need someone to cast the devil out of me… for real!

Right before I started writing this devo today (2012), I read a blog written by one of my best friends. He's on a 16-month journey with a long-time brother in Christ who is suffering with pancreatic cancer.[2] Yeah, it's not good.

You don't have to read much online to be convinced of how aggressive that particular brand of cancer can be and what it steals from its host. So, he's been fighting it. Chemo primarily. The man is doing what he can do, and there have been glimpses of hope, but he's tired and wonders at times if this is the right fight any longer?

My best friend spends his life giving counsel and offering discipleship to a wide variety of individuals. The truth is the truth, right? But here he is on this journey with a man trying to sort out a future for his wife and kids, with a real possibility he won't be here this time next year.[2] Even for a seasoned minister, that's a lot of pressure! But I love how these two men are handling it.

Most men hate to talk! But while they're both terrified of what the future holds, they're still submitted to truth and loyal accountability all the way to the end. So, they have to talk!

Most of us would rather wrestle with our crap internally, but too often the residue of that unresolved agitation trickles to the surface in character and behavioral attitudes. So, a real conversation among men has us laying swords of truth into each other. Those uncomfortable (but legitimate) questions have to be asked.

"Did you know that when you do this (fill in the blank), it gives an impression to those trying to serve you that you are not thankful for them?"

Or... how about this:

"Do you realize how harsh your tone is with your wife (husband) and kids when you're focused on one thing and they need to interrupt you?"

Those two questions could be on the table just about every time men or women get together.

If one of the terms of the relationship is honesty, then both parties are bound by honor to be honest. We can't let being sick, jobless, poor, mistreated or discriminated against determine our demeanor or joy. We can still smile. We can be courteous. We can be grateful for the kindest and smallest acts of service.

A *"joyful"* heart happens because we've made the choice to allow one of the fruits of His Spirit to flow through us! Joy is a medicine. Let's make the decision to be "full of life" during what little time we have here.

In The Pages

How are you when you're sick? Do you say "thank you" often? Sometimes this is the stuff that has to be decided when you're well. What message do you want to send in your weakness?

I'll add a few extra questions for you today: How self-aware are you when it comes to how you deal with friends, family and people in general? Do you vent through your wounds? Are you really a safe place for people to be unguarded and caring? If you're spewing poisoned pain on a regular basis, you've got to do something about what is inside you. Get back into grace. It's the ultimate reset of our life.—MDP 2018

Handful of Power

April 18
Proverbs 18

"Death and life are in the power of the tongue: and they that love it shall eat the fruit thereof." Proverbs 18:21, KJV

BAAAMMM! There it is! Out there... raw... real... bold... brutish and unapologetic in its declaration:

Death and life are in the power of the tongue!

I assume we can appreciate it this way. There is no denying the truth of this Proverb.

Like me, I'm sure you've had to dig yourself out of a bad situation on more than one occasion because you said too much, said too little, said the wrong thing or said the right thing at the wrong time and it complicated your life.

There are close to 50 verses in Proverbs that give some sort of instruction, correction or warning about the importance of stewarding our words and the use of our tongue. Nothing shines light on our internal crap like the external projection of our words.

What we so often fail to realize, even in the honest conveyance of ideas, is the potential for our words to shape thoughts, touch emotions and even steer the direction of another person's life! Words go deep inside people. So deep that it can make or break them. That's why we get such strong instruction from the Apostle Paul about our thoughts and our words.

WE CAN BE ABSOLUTELY DERAILED BY WORDS AND THOUGHTS THAT ARE NOT CONDUCIVE TO OUR HEALTH AND WHOLENESS!

"See to it that no one takes you captive through philosophy and empty deception, according to the tradition of men, according to the elementary principles of the world, rather than according to Christ" (Colossians 2:8, NASB).

"We are destroying speculations and every lofty thing raised up against the knowledge of God, and we are taking every thought captive to the obedience of Christ" (2 Corinthians 10:5, NASB).

Paul is reminding the church that there is an awesome power in words and the ideas they convey. So we're instructed to pay attention to both the words we receive into our spirits and the words we project into the spirits of those around us.

The Hebrew word for *"power"* is **yâd** (pronounced **"yawd"**), and it refers to *"a hand."* Thus indicating *"power in your hand, means in your hand and the direction determined by your hand."*

Peterson nails it:

"Words kill, words give life; they're either poison or fruit—you choose" (Proverbs 18:21, MSG).

See, now we're back to choice! We have a choice about how our words, thoughts and ideas are going to land on another person's life. Our careless words can kill their hope, their ability to desire and even destroy the faith they have for something better than what they possess.

OR we can choose to speak and prophesy life into their hopes, desires and faith! What an awesome power we have in the choice directives of our tongue!

"He who guards his mouth and his tongue, guards his soul from troubles" (Proverbs 21:23, KJV).

Very little has ever been spoken that is more true than this!

In The Pages

Have you ever weighed the thought that your tongue has the power of life or death? What do you consider a curse? What makes a blessing a blessing? How well do you speak over your own body and life? Family and friends?

Shiftless

April 19
Proverbs 19

"Laziness brings on deep sleep, and the shiftless man goes hungry." Proverbs 19:15, NIV

"Life collapses on loafers; lazybones go hungry." Proverbs 19:15, MSG

I love this imagery of the *"shiftless man."* Whatever gear he's in, that is where he stays. He won't shift up or down; he just operates inside the preconditioned, boring ways in which he is rutted.

I kind of get it (even though it wears me out), how an older man or woman might make a conscious decision to just "ride it out" to the end. Hold on to what they've got, stake out their little plot of ground, play it safe. Maybe life has knocked them upside their heads one too many times and they've decided to play it safe from here on out.

The textual context here is about food and provision. Paul also weighs in:

"For even when we were with you, we used to give you this order: if anyone is not willing to work, then he is not to eat, either. For we hear that some among you are leading an undisciplined life, doing no work at all, but acting like busybodies. Now such persons we command and exhort in the Lord Jesus Christ to work in quiet fashion and eat their own bread" (2 Thessalonians 3:10-12, NASB).

It's still a good word and worth noting. Whether it's food or provision—whichever we need—everyone appreciates the hard worker who can ramp up the exertion when necessary. But another verse concerning the ways of Christ's followers caught my attention for today.

The Apostle Peter mentions that part of his calling is to help the Body "shift" some gears. He says,

"I consider it right, as long as I am in this earthly dwelling, to stir you up by way of reminder, knowing that the laying aside of my earthly dwelling is imminent, as also our Lord Jesus Christ has made clear to me. And I will also be diligent that at any time after my departure you will be able to call these things to mind" (2 Peter 1:13-15, NASB).

In short he is saying, *"Folks, it is my job to make an impression on you that will last long after I am gone. I know you're tired of me poking on you about this stuff, but I'm under orders from the Lord and I am trying to get you to shift into another gear instead of just idling in the parking lot!"*

If you go back and review Peter's words in verses 1-12, you'll notice that he was "stirring" them and reminding the whole bunch about their callings. He believed that time was short and there were only so many days for any of them to fulfill the missions of their lives.

It's easy to concur. No one is guaranteed another day! The Kingdom was happening right then, just like it's happening right now, so Peter was encouraging them strongly to get on with it!

I love this kind of challenge! We've got stuff to do! Heaven awaits, but people do not know about the love of God, orphans need to be loved, widows need strength and the body needs encouragement. There is plenty for every one of us to do! Let's get to work!

In The Pages

When is the last time you "shifted" your spiritual gears? Who are you encouraging to pick up the pace? What would a casual observer say about your spiritual rhythm and pace for life? How much navel gazing is enough?

Deep Stripes

April 20
Proverbs 20

"Blows that hurt cleanse away evil, as do stripes the inner depths of the heart." Proverbs 20:30, NKJV

In the early 1900s, there was a revivalist from England who had a unique way of dealing with the infirmities of his attendees. Smith Wigglesworth is still considered one of the greatest healing evangelists to ever preach the Word. He is credited with raising 23 people from the dead, thousands got healed in his meetings and God only knows how many people said "yes" to Christ because of Wigglesworth's influence.

I remember the first time I heard a ministry team from Sierra Leone pray for a sick person. Holy smokes, what a racket! Evidently, evil spirits are deaf! I also saw that same team minister to a small child in a wheelchair. Their tender way of handling this child was the very breath of God. It was absolutely incredible!

Wigglesworth was known to flat-out punch you where your ailment was manifest. He would hit people so hard, he either knocked them out or else they were out under the influence of the Holy Spirit.

Wigglesworth was often asked why he hit people who came to him for help. *"I'm not hitting them. I'm hitting the devil who torments them."* Wow! That would really go over well in the American church. Sinus infection, you say? *"Hey Darryl, are you still suffering with those hemorrhoids?"* No one would ever come forward publicly for ministry again!

In Mel Gibson's epic movie, *The Passion*, there is a scene where Christ is beaten with the hell whips of Roman punishment. I've seen the movie twice, and that's enough. The imagery is lasting. Although we're generally familiar with how the punishment was administered, I'm not sure we really get it.

Jesus would have looked like raw hamburger meat when the soldiers were done with him. The part of the movie that has always stuck with me was when his mother and Mary stayed behind after the whipping to wipe up the blood from the street with a cloth. The first time I saw the scene, I truly believe the Lord said to me, *"Waste not one drop of the blood."*

I know today's Proverb is more about discipline, but I felt it necessary to revisit Isaiah 53:5: *"But he was wounded for our transgressions, He was bruised for our iniquities: the chastisement of our peace was upon him; and with His stripes we are healed"* (NASB).

It wasn't just a bad dream or a tragic story. Jesus of Nazareth accomplished much in that brutal agony. Those nails were more than spikes of death. His piercing and shedding of blood was for our deep healing and everlasting salvation!

His wounds, stripes and bruises were not for naught! We are great benefactors of such a magnificent love. Our hearts should explode in humble gratitude and overwhelming thanks at every remembrance!

In The Pages

How do you best say "thank you" for that which you can never repay? How deeply have you allowed His blood to seep into the belly of your heart? How healed are you?

V-I-C-T-O-R-Y!

April 21
Proverbs 21

"The horse is prepared for the day of battle, but victory belongs to the Lord." Proverbs 21:31, NASB

"Some boast in chariots and some in horses, but we will boast in the name of the Lord, our God." Psalms 20:7, NASB

"A horse is a false hope for victory; nor does it deliver anyone by its great strength." Psalms 33:17, NASB

"Woe to those who go down to Egypt for help and rely on horses, and trust in chariots because they are many and in horsemen because they are very strong, but they do not look to the Holy One of Israel, nor seek the Lord!" Isaiah 31:1, NASB

I love these verses for what they do inside of my heart! They confirm that God has a say in what goes on in our lives.

Oh, the images of a skinny kid and his sling, Gideon's trumpets, Israel shouting down the walls at Jericho, or Jehoshaphat's singers! You just get the sense that God is more interested in victory that we would ever surmise. While the safe bet is on the side with the most firepower, it seems God has taken up the cause of the underdog and played His trump card.

You can even find situations in scripture where God actually used Israel's own enemies to punish and discipline Israel's stubborn hard-heartedness (2 Kings 17:18-19; 2 Kings 24:2-4). Win, lose or draw, it's cool that God messes with His people—whether we like it or not. The lesson here is not about winning. It's about the fact that He moves.

Back when I was a coach, we had a motto in the weight room: **"Bigger, Faster, Stronger."** We believed those were the key components to victory. And, in sports, this is usually the case until you run up against a team with more character, discipline or heart than you.

You see... there are things going on under the surface that have a drastic impact on any outcome. External virtue is good, but it might not be enough. That is kind of the point of today's text.

You can put your confidence in the strength of man or the wonder of natural ability, but there are spiritual dynamics at play that rarely ever get noticed by mankind. I believe God is much more involved than we realize.

He's not a controller, and we are not his puppets, but He does get emotionally involved and engaged in our affairs when He wants to. He gives us a choice. He sends us messages. He wants good for us. That's something in life I don't want to miss out on.

I don't want to overlook the deeper strength. I want the help. What man can do is amazing, but God ultimately created us to love Him back.

I don't want to substitute my confidence in God's love for me for what appears to be visual stability. *"For we walk by faith, not by sight"* (2 Corinthians 5:7, NASB). That focuses our trust on something other than the strength of what we can see or touch!

In The Pages

Why do you think college and professional athletes point to the sky when they do something noteworthy? Do you ever see them point to the sky when they blow a play or fumble the ball? Do you think God cares about sports at all?

The 5th Saying

April 22
Proverbs 22

"Do you see a man skilled in his work? He will serve before kings; he will not serve before obscure men" Proverbs 22:29, NIV.

The Bible Knowledge Commentary reminds us that between Proverbs 22:17 and Proverbs 24:34, we find an assortment of 30 sayings gathered here by Solomon from the ancient voices of Egyptian wisdom well before his time. "Sayings of the wise" tend to have an element of reliability. Today, we look at the 5th saying.

I subscribe to several marketing and business babble blogs. I'm really not that in to the technical aspects, but from time to time, I read material that appropriately applies to ministry management; more specifically, people management. I have to plow through all the strategy of personal promotion, branding and self-inflation to get to what I'm really interested in. *How well do we really treat our customers? How much responsibility are we willing to take with the people who buy our stuff?* It's amazing to me how much of the discussion actually applies to ministry!

Thinking about today's verse, I immediately thought about aggressive men or women with strategic business models and big demands, and then I'm quickly moved in my spirit to see that guy or gal who pastors "The Little Flock Church" in some simple building out on some deserted road in the middle of nowhere. I mean the only marketing strategy they have is to redo the paint job on the 5x5 metal sign out in front of the church.

He or she preaches Sunday morning, Sunday night, and does a Bible study on Wednesday morning for the "Sisters Against Smut Alliance." They love as best as they can. Preachers go to the nursing home more than they care to, they drives 20 miles to the small county hospital to visit sick folk, they do four times as many funerals as weddings, and they can usually count on a big crowd of almost 70 people on Easter Sunday.

I know these preachers all too well! I know what they're thinking: *"Does God have a clue that I'm even here? What am I doing wrong? Where are all the important people? Is this all there is for me? Is obscurity my fate?"*

I was in the middle of one of these private discussions many years ago when He spoke gently, *"My sheep are sons and daughters, VIPs, kings and queens! I'd be honored if you took care of them for me."* That pretty much took care of my infatuation with numbers and posturing for appearance sake.

Ancient wisdom suggests that faithful attention to our skills development will be recognized on earth. I propose to you that heaven notices also.

In The Pages

How hard are you working on you natural skills development? What kind of natural dividends is it paying? Do you believe any of it has spiritual ramifications? How so? Is what you do "just work," or do you see Kingdom investment in what you do?

Kinsman Redeemer

April 23
Proverbs 23

"Do not move an ancient boundary stone or encroach on the fields of the fatherless, for their Defender is strong; he will take up their case against you." Proverbs 23:10-11, NIV

"As for me, I know that my Redeemer lives, and at the last He will take His stand on the earth." Job 19:25, NASB

I've never had this interview with God, but I suspect He is happiest when He gets to be Father. When we recognize him as Father, we relate to him as Father and we open ourselves up to receive his Fatherly love. Surely, this is what makes Him happy!

I know He's busy, with lots going on, and though I rarely think of Him being upset or agitated, I'm sure He gets "frothed" from time to time. When we come across passages like todays, I think God has to get pissed. I really do.

Mistreatment of orphans, taking advantage of the defenseless, exploiting the poor and the overall thumbing our noses at any kind of injustice just can't be good with Him. Solomon frequently reminds us that God will eventually set these kinds of wrongs right.

Whatever it is we think we might be getting away with is only a temporary reality. Go to your *Strong's Concordance* and take a look at the word "vengeance." Whoa! There is some strong language associated with that word.

Paul refers us back to Deuteronomy 32:35 on two separate occasions. In Hebrews 10:30-31 (if Paul is indeed the author of Hebrews), he says,

"For we know Him who said, 'Vengeance is Mine, I will repay.' And again, 'The Lord will judge His people.' It is a terrifying thing to fall into the hands of the living God" (NASB).

And again,

Romans 12:18-19, Paul says, *"If possible, so far as it depends on you, be at peace with all men. Never take your own revenge, beloved, but leave room for the wrath of God, for it is written, 'Vengeance is Mine, I will repay,' says the Lord"* (NASB).

It kind of makes me wonder if the Lady of Justice is blindfolded because she can't bear to see the aftereffects of retribution once God moves to right the wrongs we're warned about in today's Proverb?

This truth was deeply instilled in Solomon, as well as many other wisdom writers. Part of his own discernment package was the ability to administer equitable solutions among the people. He would have been heavily schooled from his own father's writings (Psalms 10:14-15, 17-18; 68:5; 82:3; and 146:9).

God is the ULTIMATE *Defender*, the *Kinsman Redeemer*, the *Protector*, the *Advocate* and the ***gō'ēl***—which was *"a family member who was personally responsible for meeting the needs of a relative who was being mistreated or taken advantage of by the unscrupulous."*

Ultimately, they (*the fatherless*) are not alone. God notices how the helpless are "handled" and will ultimately execute his justice on their behalf!

In The Pages

What happens in your spirit-man when you sense the Father's passion towards those who are less fortunate and needy? Do you believe that justice will be served? Does any aspect of this discussion offend you? Explain.

Stay Your Hand

April 24
Proverbs 24

"Don't testify against your neighbor for no good reason. Don't say things that are false. Don't say, "I'll get even; I'll do to him what he did to me." Proverbs 24:28-29, NCV

"Don't talk about your neighbors behind their backs—no slander or gossip, please. Don't say to anyone, 'I'll get back at you for what you did to me. I'll make you pay for what you did!'" Proverbs 24:28-29, MSG

It wasn't that long ago the Lord reminded me that regardless of how I was being treated in a situation, I was still personally responsible for how I conducted myself. This particular situation was absolutely unjust. The Lord told me it was unjust, with no real clear indication of how He was going to handle it, but I wasn't released to take the matter into my own hands. So, I had to back away from my own desire to "even the score."

You might be asking, "How did God tell you this?" Quite simply, I had a dream. The symbols were easy to interpret, the faces were clear and the actual message could not be mistaken.

The Lord made it clear He did not want me to handle the situation the way I had intended. I needed to take a step back, disengage and go another direction. No questions, no doubt. He had spoken.

The instructions were crystal clear and I was more than willing to take a back seat. But the real relief was that the Lord clearly identified the other party as being in the wrong. Indeed, He had seen the unfair position that I had been put in, but it was His place to rectify the situation—not mine.

I can't tell you how comforting it was to know that He had seen the whole thing, and He was going to handle it. As irritating as that situation had been, that dream released me from all internal turmoil. To continue to harp on it or even respond when asked about the whole nasty business brought a drudgery and tiredness to my spirit. It was now dead to me. No reason to keep dragging that around.

Today's verses are good counsel for us. We get so wound up and defensive, we forget that God sees everything. If it's truly unjust, God has noticed and He's got a plan. Behold the strength of the Lord! He WILL move—in *His* way and *His* timing.

In The Pages

What are the lessons you've learned about God's knowledge of injustice? Has He ever stayed your hand when you wanted to hit back? Did you blow past the warning, or did you withdraw? How did it turn out for you?

Expansively Aware

April 25
Proverbs 25

"As the heavens are high and the earth is deep, so the hearts of kings are unsearchable." Proverbs 25:3, NIV

"What's the matter with you? I think your brain's going soft with all those women! Never tell anybody outside the family what you're thinking again." Don Corleone, The Godfather

If you took all the examples of mankind's foolishness from the Wisdom sayings, you'd find that most of them fall into three primary categories. The first of these is about **our getting in a hurry and not thinking things through before we act**. The second involves the **sorrow of exploring life with a weak morality**. The third is our **insistence on having our own way**.

The overall message here is that we have a responsibility to pay attention to our surroundings. We can't be impervious because we're unaware. We were all created for purpose and it requires we pay attention to details.

In Solomon's day, the common man would have little understanding (if any) of the pressures and responsibilities of being King. Any attention you got from him was not to be taken for granted. Favor was to be relished and stewarded with great care.

The King always had other fish frying. If you happened to see him play a card, it didn't mean you knew what was in his hand. Just being in the King's presence demanded precision down to the smallest details. A fool wouldn't think about any of this—and that would be a major problem.

So may I ask you a few questions?

How well do you pay attention when it comes to the people who help steward your soul or your spiritual development—your elders or your leaders? Has it dawned on you that they might have a few things going on in their lives besides the problems you're dealing with?

Do you add value to them by attempting to peek into their lives? When was the last time you bought their lunch, their coffee... surprised them with their favorite bottle of wine or perfume?

Quite frankly, younger generations are more prone to taking than giving, especially (and unfortunately) when it comes to spiritual sons and daughters with their spiritual parents and mentors. People who have been in the "disciple-making and mentoring business" for a while know that it is better to give than to receive. That is why they do what they do.

They are very in touch with who their source of strength is. They are more motivated by love than by anything else, so the fact that they love on you, tell you the truth, regardless of how much it hurts, hold you, but not grab you, is a great indicator that they're not looking for some kind of repayment.

BUT, that's all the more reason for us to "give back" something to the people who pour into us. It is foolish to not pay attention!

Wisdom challenges us to be expansively aware and really tapped in to every opportunity we have to sharpen our mind and shape our character. Let's be a blessing to the people (the kings and queens) who have carved a special place in their heart for you and me.

In The Pages

Let's spend some time today thinking of ways to bless the people in our lives who have poured in to us spiritually. What token of appreciation would really convey a "thank you" with genuine thoughtfulness and love?

Guns Loaded

April 26
Proverbs 26

"Like a thornbush brandished by the hand of a drunkard is a proverb in the mouth of a fool." Proverbs 26:9, NRSV

"To ask a moron to quote a proverb is like putting a scalpel in the hands of a drunk." Proverbs 26:9, MSG

I have no interest in insulting your intelligence, but may I point out the obvious here? The reason it's a bad idea for an inebriated individual to trim a rose bush is because his or her judgment and perspective is impaired.

Rose bushes are awesome when they are bloomed in beauty, but if you mishandle them for whatever reason, there are severe consequences. Again, you want your surgeon sober when he's removing your appendix. Just saying. A surgeon who is under the influence actually becomes unsafe because of what has consumed him.

Like the rose bush or the scalpel, a proverb isn't the problem. It's any of these things in the hands of a fool that wreaks havoc and causes destruction.

So, I want to try my hand at paraphrasing today's text:

> *"A loaded gun in the hands of a lunatic is like scripture in the mouth of a bitter or legalistic Christian."*

This isn't an NRA advertisement by any means, but guns are not the whole problem in and of themselves. The fact that bad people, immature people, negligent people stockpile arsenals of assault weapons **IS A PROBLEM**.

I believe it's a good idea for law enforcement personnel to carry loaded weapons while they're on duty. I also think it's a good thing for our nation's military to be armed while actively defending our country. A thug with a gun is quite another story.

Scripture is full of life! BUT using it as a license to put people in bondage is not a good thing. Likewise, using the Bible to control how people live is a gross misusage.

I have devoted my life to serving the Lord and his people. It requires me to glean and incorporate the foundational truths and great themes of scripture. But I also must be aware that if I make the text a simple rulebook of do's and don'ts, I have killed the Spirit of love and help that is infused in the Bible.

I do not have permission to grind my way through life using scripture as the litmus test of "who's in" and "who's out," what is right and what is wrong or what is good and what is evil. What a shallow way to live life!

Honestly, there were seasons in my life where I did that. I was nothing more than a modern day Pharisee who needed to be saved from having to be right all the time! Being full of legalism and self-righteous pride made me drunk with religious zeal. I was nothing like the Jesus I was trying to serve.

The problem wasn't the scripture. **I WAS THE PROBLEM.** We need to take some time to make sure we are using scripture correctly and safely.

In The Pages

Do you use scripture to make your point in religious altercations? How often do you use scripture to scold another person's bad behavior? How consumed are you with having right doctrine? Who ultimately gets to decide whether your doctrine is right or wrong?

Love Rebukes

April 27
Proverb 27

"It is better to correct someone openly than to have love and not show it." Proverbs 27:5, NCV

"He who rebukes a man will in the end gain more favor than he who has a flattering tongue." Proverbs 28:23, NIV

"[Love] takes pleasure in the flowering of truth." 1 Corinthians 13:6, MSG

I think we all pee ourselves just a little bit when we think about either giving or receiving a rebuke. Maybe you've been in an altercation with a Christian brother or sister that left a bad taste in your mouth?

If you look at the Hebrew and Greek, there are a wide variety of reasons for a rebuke. It's not all about bringing a harsh correction, which seems to be our default understanding. There is so much more involved than just pointing out an error or a weakness. With rebuking someone comes the responsibility to also restore and set back in proper order.

How a person rebukes has everything to do with the real motivation for sorting out the problem.

True discipleship is laced with the loving insertion of opposing thoughts and ideas, which ultimately benefit the one being discipled. It doesn't have to be loud, stern or "in your face". Remember it's an exercise to shine the light of truth on something broke.

Wisdom would rather we risk wounding someone we really care about, than ignore a real problem to avoid "rocking the boat." Believers who love deeply tell each other the truth. Feedback is part of healthy communication and growth.

Living things shit. It's a fact. It gets messy sometimes, but loving relationships require honest communication. To only ignore problems in a relationship and "hold one another at arm's length" eventually destroys trust.

In Galatians 2:11-21 we see a fascinating encounter! Our great common hero, Peter, had been the benefactor of a great revelation: Gentiles were no longer to be estranged from the Grace of God and the empowering of the Holy Spirit. What a revelation!

But sometimes those old religious ideas would creep back into Peter's way of life. Paul, the new kid on the block, was highly educated, articulate and more than eager to argue his ideas. And although Paul could have lost his cool, I suspect his great respect for the Original Twelve is what restrained him when he confronted them.

Paul loved and admired those people. Sometimes I wonder if the actual altercation was as harsh as the ink indicates. Regardless of details, Paul got the job done because of what was at stake. We should all be thankful that rebuke happened! In short, we'd all be screwed if this way of thinking had gone unopposed.

In The Pages

How do you prepare when you have to bring correction to a peer? What is your response when you get corrected? Have you ever blown an attempt to rebuke someone? Did you fix it?

The Deeper Issue

April 28
Proverbs 28

"He who keeps the law is a discerning son, but he who is a companion of gluttons humiliates his father." Proverbs 28:7, NASB

There are over 230 references to the Hebrew word **nachălâh** (pronounced *nakh-al-aw´*) in the Old Testament. It means, *"inheritance."*

If there was any thing the Hebrew people understood, it was the concept of inheritance. It was what most of their decision-making revolved around. Everyone in the family was entitled to a portion of the estate. And everyone had a responsibility to further those capital investments as best they could.

No one was excluded from passing down the blessing to the next generation. It was just the way it was. Your life was merely a set-up for your children, and their children, and their children's children.

The implied concept was simple:

> **1. Today has a direct impact on tomorrow**
>
> **2. Invest today for future fruit**
>
> **3. Curses and blessings alike are passed down the family bloodline**
> *(just like human DNA).*

Everyone understood the deal!

I don't think what Lady Wisdom is suggesting in today's text is just about "keeping the rules". Nor am I convinced the rowdy friends are the problem. The fact that the son or daughter is even attracted to such recklessness or lack of personal self-discipline is probably more at the heart of this warning.

It would be wise to refer back to Proverbs 23:20-21 and make a fortified case for the perils of such lack of discipline. That should be enough to motivate most parents to warn their children about such a lifestyle.

The *humiliation* today's text is referring to isn't necessarily because of how a child is behaving, but because of the messages that behavior—that loose lifestyle—conveys to an entire society.

This word for *"gluttons"* means a lot more than a person's tendency to pig out at the pizza buffet or local pub. The word is packed with all kinds of moral deficiency. In the mind of a regular citizen of ancient Israel, a glutton was a wayward person, a prodigal or a person who had turned his back on prudent stewardship.

Remember, an inheritance required a life-long commitment from all parties involved. A glutton is someone who says to society, to tradition, *"To hell with all of that!"* It was almost unthinkable, and any kid who succumbed to this way of thinking brought quite a bit of shame to the family.

Over and over and over again, Wisdom asks us to take an honest peek inside our hearts and evaluate how our today is affecting our tomorrow. It is really good counsel for all of us.

In The Pages

How much of your life involves stewarding something to be passed down to generations after you? How regularly do you assess the quality of your stewardship? What is the inheritance you want to really pass on?

Hush It

April 29
Proverbs 29

"Do you see people who speak too quickly? There is more hope for a foolish person than for them." Proverbs 29:20, NCV

"In the exercise of His will He brought us forth by the word of truth, so that we would be a kind of first fruits among His creatures. This you know, my beloved brethren. But everyone must be quick to hear, slow to speak and slow to anger;

for the anger of man does not achieve the righteousness of God." James 1:18-20, NASB

"Post this at all the intersections, dear friends: Lead with your ears, follow up with your tongue, and let anger straggle along in the rear." James 1:19, MSG

I've included Peterson's translation (The Message) in today's devotional because I didn't want you to miss out on the brilliance of what he offers.

This is at the heart of today's lesson!

Sometimes, one has to really nestle down with a verse in order to think through what the writer is saying. With all the references to the word "fool" throughout Proverbs, this one actually suggests that the fool is in a better position to receive grace than the person who knows better than to shoot his mouth off in a moment of lost composure, but does it anyway.

James clearly points out that the Lord has put intentionality in His plans towards his sons and daughters. We (that's me, you, us—the church) are the *"first fruits,"* given as a pledge, in order to bring in the entire harvest. It's brilliant imagery! And James goes on to point out that it matters greatly how those first fruits are to relate to the rest of God's creatures.

First fruits were to be consumed. It was an offering that meshed faith with hard work. That particular bread, grain, fruit, whatever was being offered, was given to the Lord. What came through sweat and toil was given generously and freely. There was a sacred trust that once these first fruits left a farmer's hand, the priest would immediately sanctify them and use them as the Law directed. This is all in the imagery of what James was referring to in today's passage.

We are God's *"first fruits,"* and He trusts us to be consumed by the nations of the earth. How we present ourselves affects whether or not we are received and consumed.

Not too long ago, I got pretty upset at a seemingly senseless situation. It's been a long time since I can remember being that angry. In a supposedly candid conversation, I let all of my inflamed anger and passion spill out of me. Even with the "off the record" guarantee, it was too much information, too brutal, too real—and some of what I said in anger wasn't even how I really felt.

In short, my mouth was working overtime when it should have been taking a nap! Yes, I repented later, but some of that foul goop will never make it back inside the tube. Sometimes, it's just better to stay quiet.

In The Pages

What are your thoughts about today's lesson? Where do you identify? When was the last time you were hurt by someone else's words?

The Name of His Son

April 30
Proverbs 30

"The sayings of Agur son of Jakeh—an oracle: This man declared to Ithiel, to Ithiel and to Ucal: "I am the most ignorant of men; I do not have a man's understanding. I have not learned wisdom, nor have I knowledge of the Holy One. Who has gone up to heaven and come down? Who has gathered up the wind in the hollow of his hands? Who has wrapped up the waters in his cloak? Who has established all the ends of the earth? What is his name, and the name of his son? Tell me if you know!" Proverbs 30:1-4, NIV

I've been a squatter today. Nope, that's not a bathroom update. I've really pondered about what I'm supposed to do with this passage of scripture.

I tried to jump elsewhere, but I kept feeling the Lord wanted it exposed today. The commentators aren't much help. They don't know the true identity of *Agur, Jakeh, Ithiel* or *Ucal*.

The Proverb is written with a perspective of irony that reeks of Job-*ish* type taunts and anthropomorphic dialogue. This guy is not ignorant. Of course he has studied and learned wisdom. Of course He knows God! Of course!

Already knowing the answer to all five of these questions, Agur prophetically unleashes the magnificent confidence of a man who has speculated on the expansion of the all-encompassing influence of Jehovah. The question that holds prophetic weight is the fifth question: *"What is his name, and the name of his son?"* Agur is looking past his literal name to something much deeper.

The Hebrew word for *"name"* is **shêm** (pronounced *shame*). Indeed, it conveys the idea of *"position and individuality,"* but it also implies *"honor, authority and character,"* thus revealing the nature of a thing. Agur understood that unless God had revealed Himself to us, we couldn't have ever known him (verse 4).

Elsewhere, in another time, another book, Job's friend confirms this notion:

"Do you think you can explain the mystery of God? Do you think you can diagram God Almighty? God is far higher than you can imagine, far deeper than you can comprehend, stretching farther than earth's horizons, far wider than the endless ocean" (Job 11:7-9, MSG).

The Apostle Paul agrees:

"Oh, the depth of the riches both of the wisdom and knowledge of God! How unsearchable are His judgments and unfathomable His ways!" (Romans 11:33, NASB).

Without divine revelation, we can know *of* Him, but we can't really *know Him*.

Then he mentions *"the name of his son,"* which was going to be the ultimate revealing. Jesus, God with skin, walking among mere mortals, showing us the nature and fullness of God's pure and spotless nature!

Paul wrote,

"For it was the Father's good pleasure for all the fullness to dwell in Him" (Colossians 1:19, NASB), and *"For in Him all the fullness of Deity dwells in bodily form"* (Colossians 2:9, NASB).

Have we not benefited from the open view of love through Jesus Christ? Did we not first taste the Father's love for us through that atoning sacrifice? Have we not understood the prophetic implications of Emmanuel, God with us?

Why YES, of course we have!

The prophet Micah foretold of the revealing of the son.

"But as for you, Bethlehem Ephrathah, too little to be among the clans of Judah, from you One will go forth for Me to be ruler in Israel. **His goings forth are from long ago, from the days of eternity.***" Therefore He will give them up until the time when she who is in labor has borne a child. Then the remainder of His brethren will return to the sons of Israel. And He will arise and shepherd His flock in the strength of the Lord, in the majesty of the name of the Lord His God. And they will remain, because at that time He will be great to the ends of the earth"* (Micah 5:2-4, NASB).

From the beginning of time, His name has been, and will forever be, **Jesus**, our Messiah, our Lord, our King, THE Christ!

In The Pages

If Jesus' nature is the same as God's nature, what attributes of character do you ascribe to them both?

She Is Pushy!

May 1
Proverbs 1

"Simpletons! How long will you wallow in ignorance? Cynics! How long will you feed your cynicism? Idiots! How long will you refuse to learn?" Proverbs 1:22, MSG

I want to leave you with one thought today: Lady Wisdom calls out! She goes out in the street, stands in the middle of traffic, and shouts (Proverbs 1:20-21)!

There is something in God's heart that won't allow Him to leave us alone when it comes to things in our lives that are not beneficial to us. I would propose to you that this is real evidence of His love for us. Yes, God loves us. Like, *personally* loves us.

He's much more interested in being our Father and less inclined to treat us as soldiers who are under command to obey at all cost. He's after the relationship, not just our sacrifice and obedience.

Some scholars believe that today's Proverb is actually the prophetic voice of Jesus engaging mankind. Check out the similarity:

*"For this reason also **the wisdom of God said**, 'I will send to them prophets and apostles, and some of them they will kill and some they will persecute, so that the blood of all the prophets, shed since the foundation of the world, may be charged against this generation, from the blood of Abel to the blood of Zechariah, who was killed between the altar and the house of God; yes, I tell you, it shall be charged against this generation'"* (Luke 11:49-51, NASB).

There is more going on here than just a rebuke, although love can be in a rebuke. Lady Wisdom is "calling out" to make known her desire that wholeness and blessing follow her subjects.

Wisdom isn't pestering us—she's exposing herself. The only reason for anyone's feathers to be ruffled here is if we haven't been paying attention. So, let's turn our heads, tune our ears and take a look at our lives.

Every time I read one of these verbal explosions in Proverbs, I have to check myself to see if I'm being personally addressed here. Frankly, that's the point. And I've come to the peaceful realization that the Spirit of God has no issue pointing out the small warts and gashes that cling to my personality. I've learned to be cool with that. If left unchecked, they impose a real strain on the relationships I really care about, and that is NOT cool!

It's a good thing when Lady Wisdom is hollering in the streets!

In The Pages

Do you ever ask yourself if you are the one being addressed in these kinds of verses? Are you selectively naïve when you don't want to deal with an issue? What are you cynical about right now? What do you need to brush up on that's been on the back burner for way too long?

The Ecstasy of Discretion

May 2
Proverbs 2

"Discretion will preserve you; understanding will keep you, to deliver you from the way of evil, from the man who speaks perverse things." Proverbs 2:11-12, NKJV

This word *"discretion"* is an incredibly beautiful word! The commentators of the NET Bible describe discretion as *"the ability to know the best course of action for achieving one's goals. It is knowledge and understanding with a purpose. This kind of knowledge enables a person to make choices that will protect him from blunders and their consequences."*

I like the way Solomon sets it up here to be almost dual purposed. *Discretion* helps you to maneuver your way as you go out, but it also protects you from those out there who seek to hurt you. No matter where you find yourself, discretion has got you covered—north, south, east and west!

Solomon uses the word *discretion* seven different times in Proverbs to paint his instructions. Honestly, I think the King was absolutely marinated in the stuff.

Solomon finally gets worked up about building the Temple and a new palace for himself. His father had suffered personal agony in not being able to pull it off, so for Solomon, everything had to be right.

The first thing he did was write to a general contractor and solicit his favor which allowed him to hire all the skilled labor that was necessary to build

God's house. Again, the crème in Solomon rose to the top, and he sent a letter to Huram, King of Tyre, to solicit his help in the project.

A quick peek at Huram's response speaks volumes about Solomon's gracious effect on people:

"Then Huram, king of Tyre, answered in a letter sent to Solomon: "Because the Lord loves His people, He has made you king over them." Then Huram continued, "Blessed be the Lord, the God of Israel, who has made heaven and earth, who has given King David a wise son, endowed with **discretion and understanding***, who will build a house for the Lord and a royal palace for himself"* (2 Chronicles 2:11-12, NASB).

When discretion is applied generously, it usually bears much fruit!

If you'll take a moment and continue reading (2 Chronicles 2:13-18), you'll see what the beautiful return for discretion looks like!

In The Pages

OK, so you are a brilliant person. But did you ever stop to think about how you know the things that you know? Was it all mechanically learned, or was any of your knowledge imposed by something other than academics and experience? What do you think Huram meant by referring to Solomon's discretion and understanding as *endowed*?

Terror Of Suddenness

May 3
Proverbs 3

"Be not afraid of sudden fear, neither of the desolation of the wicked, when it cometh. For the Lord shall be thy confidence, and shall keep thy foot from being taken." Proverbs 3:25-26, KJV

Back in my seminary days, I memorized scripture on little cards that I acquired from The Navigators. They were all printed in the King's old language. While I've always preached out of the NASB, I like to check the KJV to see what words might pop up in that particular translation.

Today, the word *"desolation"* does it for me. It's not a word we hear too often in today's culture. Webster defines it as *"complete emptiness or destruction, anguished misery or loneliness."* That doesn't quite convey what Solomon is talking about here.

The NASB actually does a better job of conveying the idea in contemporary terms:

"Do not be afraid of sudden fear nor of the onslaught of the wicked when it comes" (Proverbs 3:25, NASB).

"Onslaught" means *"false reports, false speech, and or schemes to bring the "terror of suddenness" to the innocent."* This is colorful language most people my age can really identify with.

We older generations have been through some stuff. Most of us can relate to that sudden feeling of dread and terror that comes with a bad report, or when someone makes false accusations about your character or your intentions. What's really tough is that it requires a lot of emotional work to defend such nonsense. It can be extremely draining, and even costly, to fight back, especially if the chances of really rectifying the situation are slim.

Today's Proverb is valuable because it gives us hope. God sees everything, and He knows the truth. He says to be courageous, and He'll give us what we need to weather the storm.

Scripture teaches us that not all battles are won with conventional warfare. Plenty of blood has been spilled over the ages as altercations among nations have motivated men to arms! But the real battles we face are spiritual, and what's at stake is control over our mind and heart. These are the battles that are won with petition and prayer.

Paul told the Ephesians,

"For our struggle is not against flesh and blood, but against the rulers, against the powers, against the world forces of this darkness, against the spiritual forces of wickedness in the heavenly places" (Ephesians 6:12, NASB).

He encouraged them to dress themselves in *spiritual* armor because metal armor is useless in a spiritual battle.

"Not by might nor by power, but by My Spirit" (Zechariah 4:6, NASB).

HE is the source of our hope and settled confidence! Sudden terror may arise, but the Lord gives us strength to endure.

In The Pages

Is your tendency to fight your battles in the natural or by the Spirit? What is the promise in Proverbs 3:26? Job 5:21? In Hebrew, *"confidence"* means *"fatness."* What can that possibly mean?

Passing On the Good

May 4
Proverbs 4

"For I give you sound teaching; do not abandon my instruction." Proverbs 4:2, NASB

"Give ear, O heavens, and let me speak; and let the earth hear the words of my mouth. Let my teaching drop as the rain, my speech distill as the dew, as the droplets on the fresh grass and as the showers on the herb. For I proclaim the name of the Lord; ascribe greatness to our God! The Rock! His work is perfect, for all His ways are just; a God of faithfulness and without injustice, righteous and upright is He." Deuteronomy 32:1-4, NASB

In the middle of Solomon's nostalgic visit back to his childhood, he encourages his own children to tap into the *"sound teaching"* that was given to him by his father, King David. The word for *"sound"* is **ṭôwb** (pronounced *tobe)*, and it means, *"good"* in about the widest sense possible.

Solomon knew that what he had received from his dad was indeed "good," and it had served him well. Now he wanted to pass that "good" down to his own children!

That is what loving parents do—pass on the "good!"

One of the most obvious desires of the Apostle Paul was to pass on sound teaching to the young Christians he was influencing. This term frequently appears in his letters to Timothy (1 Timothy 1:10, 4:6, 6:3; 2 Timothy 1:13, 4:3).

Titus also refers to this idea of sound teaching in his letter (Titus 1:9, 1:13, 2:1-2, 2:8). Early on (and yes, still today) the church was being bombarded with unhealthy messages from false teachers who were negatively influencing the sheep. Sound teaching in this context meant *"healthy, uncorrupted, and pure."*

Paul and Titus both pointed to the Lord as being the final authority on what is pure, what is healthy, and what is uncorrupted. They were merely stewards of what they had been entrusted with (1 Thessalonians 2:4; Titus 1:3).

Doctrine is probably the greatest divider among church folk. The priesthood of the believer allows for our differences of expression and thought, but we get so bent out of shape in defending our own doctrine or in persecuting someone else's doctrine. It's almost as if the Body is in a constant gut-wrench over theological metrics.

Jesus was much more interested in heart stuff than in trying to sort out screwed up theology. I don't remember Him ever saying, "You believe wrong," though He did call the Pharisees out on their hypocritical lifestyles.

One thing is for certain:

We can't do this Kingdom stuff without having some grace and love, AND that is about as *sound* as it gets.

What good does it do us to have sound teaching if we won't live it out lovingly? Remember, He is the source of what we believe and propagate. If it really is sound, healthy, and full of Good News, it will have His heart and Spirit in it!

In The Pages

Can you explain your doctrinal positions without manifesting anger, pride, or arrogance? Why do you think the church is so divided over doctrine and belief systems? What does this do to the overall unity of the Body?

Best Seat In The House

May 5
Proverbs 5

"For the ways of man are before the eyes of the Lord, and He ponders all his paths." Proverbs 5:21, NKJV

"Therefore, since we are surrounded by such a great cloud of witnesses, let us throw off everything that hinders and the sin that so easily entangles, and let us run with perseverance the race marked out for us. Let us fix our eyes on Jesus,

the author and perfecter of our faith, who for the joy set before him endured the cross, scorning its shame, and sat down at the right hand of the throne of God. Consider him who endured such opposition from sinful men, so that you will not grow weary and lose heart." Hebrews 12:1-3, NASB

The thought I want you to carry today is that you NEVER journey alone.

God sees, understands, and is neither aloof nor unconcerned about what happens in your everyday life. He doesn't just "check-in" for the big stuff. He notices, even reflects and mulls over, everything.

If your image of God is that of a tyrant waiting to see if you make a mistake so He can dole out appropriate punishment, then this is a wearisome consideration. I'm convinced that our God, who is the very substance of love (1 John 4:8), doesn't operate like that.

Because He loves us, he won't control us. He has given us the freedom to make choices. As a result, we see bad choices end in bad consequences all the time! But just because we face consequences for poor choices—coupled with taunting from the devil—doesn't negate the love of the Father for His creation.

Yes, the overall message of Proverbs 5 is packed with warnings concerning moral infidelity, but Wisdom also encourages us to remember that we have help to overcome temptation. Again, the FATHER knows what we face! His vantage point is much greater than ours. It is wise to seek His guidance through treacherous times.

This imagery in Hebrews is awesome! Imagine heavenly bleachers spilling over with ancient eyes that watch and encourage from the best seats in the house? If the angel armies have box seats with a view, I'm certain God sees even more from the press box!

There are plenty of references in scripture that confirm God's ability to see us:

"His eyes are on the ways of men; He sees their every step" (Job 34:21, NIV).

"I obey your precepts and your statutes, for all my ways are known to you" (Psalms 119:168, NIV).

"The eyes of the Lord are everywhere, keeping watch on the wicked and the good" (Proverbs 15:3, NIV).

"My eyes are on all their ways; they are not hidden from me, nor is their sin concealed from my eyes" (Jeremiah 16:17, NIV).

"Great are your purposes and mighty are your deeds. Your eyes are open to all the ways of men..." (Jeremiah 32:19, NIV).

"Nothing in all creation is hidden from God's sight. Everything is uncovered and laid bare before the eyes of him to whom we must give account. Therefore, since we have a great high priest who has gone through the heavens, Jesus the Son of God, let us hold firmly to the faith we profess. For we do not have a high priest who is unable to sympathize with our weaknesses, but we have one who has been tempted in every way, just as we are—yet was without sin. Let us then approach the throne of grace with confidence, so that we may receive mercy and find grace to help us in our time of need" (Hebrews 4:13-16, NIV).

Oh yes, He sees! Hallelujah! Yes indeed, He sees!

In The Pages

Do you like the fact that God sees you? Does it settle you or make you nervous? In what ways has He shown you that He sees you?

Whack that Sucka

May 6
Proverbs 6

"Therefore his calamity will come suddenly; instantly he will be broken and there will be no healing." Proverbs 6:15, NASB

"So trouble will strike them in an instant; suddenly they will be so hurt no one can help them." Proverbs 6:15, NCV

"Catastrophe is just around the corner for them, a total smashup, their lives ruined beyond repair." Proverbs 6:15, MSG

"'For I know the plans that I have for you,' declares the Lord, 'plans for welfare and not for calamity to give you a future and a hope.'" Jeremiah 29:11, NASB

I added the Jeremiah passage to defuse any thought that God takes morbid pleasure in bringing trouble on anyone.

Plan "A" is for our blessing.

The church has been steeped in this unhealthy paradigm that God is this stringent disciplinarian, just waiting for us to make a mistake.

Jesus didn't show up in the "nick of time" to keep God from killing us. Jesus was actually a *part* of the love package God has for His creation. It's hard for many of us to consider the love of God, but His plans really do include hope for a blessed today and tomorrow!

Even with all of that said trouble still comes to each of us. It rains on the righteous and the unrighteous alike. The sun shines on the good and the bad. The goodness of God is available to any and all who will partake. But those who insist on living a certain way can expect repercussions of significant magnitude.

Proverbs 6:12-14 lists a number of character faults that beg for agonizing retribution. Solomon doesn't really clarify whether the repercussions come from God himself or if it's just evil being returned upon evil. Either way, one thing is for certain:

THE CONSEQUENCE IS GOING TO BE HELL ON EARTH.

There was a prophetic exercise that was common during the time Solomon wrote Proverbs. People would put the names of their enemies on a big clay pot and then whack the crap out of it with an iron rod. This would not only destroy the pot, but it would send a message that they intended the same for their enemies.

Today's Proverb uses the words *"suddenly," "strike them," "instantly," "total smashup," "broken," "ruined beyond repair,"* and *"no healing."* Solomon may have been drawing a few parallels here with the end results being less than favorable.

Wisdom is always pleading for us to consider the road ahead and avoid unnecessary danger and destruction. Today's text offers no less. Retribution comes, but is it the kind we want?

In The Pages

Is our culture really convinced that the good guy always wins, and the bad guy eventually loses? Do you believe this? Other than scripture, what else could you point to that confirms this notion that justice always prevails?

In the Evening of Day

May 7
Proverbs 7

"In the twilight, in the evening, in the middle of the night and in the darkness." Proverbs 7:9, NASB

"Others have been with those who rebel against the light; they do not want to know its ways nor abide in its paths. The murderer arises at dawn; he kills the poor and the needy, and at night he is as a thief. The eye of the adulterer waits for the twilight, saying, 'No eye will see me.' and he disguises his face. In the dark they dig into houses, they shut themselves up by day; they do not know the light. For the morning is the same to him as thick darkness, for he is familiar with the terrors of thick darkness." Job 24:13-17, NASB

From 2006 to 2009, Patti and I had the privilege of living with a beautiful elderly queen named Mary Alice.[3] Our job was simple—to keep an eye on her, help her out around the house and make sure she was safe.

We found such great joy in serving this lovely lady. We absolutely fell in love with her! And in living with her, we learned a great deal about who she was.

It didn't take long for us to discover that Mary Alice had a running battle with the dark. When the daylight would begin to fade, she'd say, *"Let's keep the dark outside."* That was our cue to shut the curtains and turn all three (100-watt) lamps on in the den where she watched TV. She kept that room as bright as possible, just the way she liked it. Darkness didn't have a prayer in there!

Obviously, today's Proverb is all about context. The problem wasn't the darkness itself, but what was going on under the cover of darkness.

The enemy likes to work in darkness. If we only think of darkness in terms of actual "night time," we might miss what Solomon is trying to say here.

Darkness also involves secrecy and clandestine operations. The Hebrew understanding for the word *"evening"* literally means *"evening of the day."*

Adultery, pornography, prostitution and **sex trafficking** aren't just nighttime activities. This stuff goes on 24/7 all over the world.

The real darkness is when our society thinks these injustices only happen in places like Thailand or India. Our religious naïveté makes us blind to what is happening right under our noses.

SEX TRAFFICKING IS A PROBLEM RIGHT HERE IN THE GOOD OLE USA!!!

By turning on the lights, we expose these problems. When enough people become aware, concern will arise and we might actually have a chance at fighting these crimes against humanity. That is part of our being *"the light of the world"* (Matthew 5:14).

OUR REMAINING BLIND AND QUIET IS NOT HELPFUL IN THESE MATTERS... AT ALL!

In The Pages

How informed are you about the problem of sex trafficking in the United States? Maybe you could take some time today to search out some information and get involved?

It All Had To Be Just Right

May 8
Proverbs 8

"When he drew a boundary for Sea, posted a sign that said no trespassing, and then staked out Earth's Foundations, I was right there with him, making sure everything fit. Day after day I was there, with my joyful applause, always enjoying his company, delighted with the world of things and creatures, happily celebrating the human family." Proverbs 8:29-31, MSG

During my three and a half years of Seminary, I would (semi-regularly) attend the Chapel service held each day on campus.[4] I had my favorite professors I wanted to hear preach, and there were sometimes other special guests (usually pastors of big churches who were very important people in the denomination), so it would usually draw a pretty big crowd of eager young students.

One day, the message was from one of our theology professors.[5] I don't remember his entire sermon that day, but I do remember that I was absolutely mesmerized.

The message had to do with the perfection of ten factors pertaining to the earth and its interrelation to the sun. Remove or alter any one of those conditions, whether it was the size of the sun, temperature of the sun, earth's distance from the sun, speed of the earth's rotation, axial tilt of the earth, composition of the earth, the effect of the moon, etc., and the possibility of sustaining life on this orb is drastically reduced, if not eliminated all together.

There was nothing combative in the spirit of the message against science or evolutionary theory. It was primarily factual and his presentation was remarkable! I remember thinking, *"Whether or not a person ever considers the possibility of intelligent design, one must admit that the infinite heavens are quite expansive. How all of this works can't just be the result of some ancient cosmic crap-shoot, can it?"*

I was in sheer wonder and total awe. All of those things he mentioned, everything had to be just right! How can we ever really get our minds wrapped around all of that?

Reading Proverbs 8 today reminded me again of Solomon's brilliant ability to paint pictures for us. As God was designing and building the heavens, innumerable galaxy systems, star complexes, and ultimately the earth, Wisdom was right there with him to applaud and celebrate each and every element of the process.

The King has again personified Lady Wisdom as a good friend, a companion of the highest regard. If this friend was good for the encouragement of the Godhead, then we too should welcome the warmth of her service. She knows some stuff!

In The Pages

How often do you think about the kinds of things my professor was talking about? What happens in your spirit when you chew on the expansiveness of God's ability? Have you ever considered that Wisdom is present when God creates? What are your thoughts about that?

Details

May 9
Proverbs 9

"The banquet meal is ready to be served: lamb roasted, wine poured out, table set with silver and flowers." Proverbs 9:2, MSG

His Banner Over Me
He brought me to His banqueting table
And His banner over me is love!
I am my beloveds and he is mine
And His banner over me is love
We can feel the love of God in this place
We believe Your goodness
We receive Your grace
We delight ourselves at your table oh God
You do all things well, just look at our lives
And His banner over me is love
His banner over you, His banner over me
His banner over us, it is love, love, love

Kevin Prosch © 1991 Mercy/Vineyard Publishing. Used by Permission.

This isn't the first time we've heard Solomon talk about this whole idea of inviting guests into the banquet hall (literally, *the wine house*) to enjoy the King's delicacies. Check this out:

The Woman *"I'm just a wildflower picked from the plains of Sharon, a lotus blossom from the valley pools".*

The Man *"A lotus blossoming in a swamp of weeds—that's my dear friend among the girls in the village".*

The Woman *"As an apricot tree stands out in the forest, my lover stands above the young men in town. All I want is to sit in his shade, to taste and savor his delicious love. He took me home with him for a festive meal, but his eyes feasted on me! Oh! Give me something refreshing to eat—and quickly! Apricots, raisins—anything. I'm about to faint with love! His left hand cradles my head, and his right arm encircles my waist!" Song of Solomon 2:1-6, MSG*

As the King entertains his new lover and places before her a spread of luxury, so does Lady Wisdom in her preparations to serve those who follow her counsel. With rich meats, special drink, and attention to every detail, her guest is promised an evening to remember!

As we journey together through the Book of Proverbs, it's easy to see that Lady Wisdom is a stickler about the small details. Today's proverb encapsulates the great care and preparation Wisdom has made to insure that every blessing afforded mankind is ready to be given, and received, for our benefit.

But let's not overlook one simple concept:

In order to enjoy the benefits of what Lady Wisdom offers, we must attend the banquet!

We have to tap in to what she has to offer. Only then do we get the insights into the things that really reveal the heart of our God.

Much like the joy that fills a mother's heart as she nurses her newborn baby, the heart of our Father is filled when we partake of the choice morsels that Wisdom offers us. Yes, Wisdom serves us, because His banner over us IS love!

In The Pages

When was the last time you sat for an elegant meal at a nice restaurant? Do you enjoy the whole experience, or are you there just for the food? What message does the server, who operates with precision, convey?

Love Blanket

May 10
Proverbs 10

"Hatred stirs up strife, but love covers all transgressions." Proverbs 10:12, NASB

I'm convinced there is nothing more confusing to the world than the message of the Gospel on the lips of people who have anger and hate in their hearts. When our attitudes and behavior are not in alignment with our theology, we come across as nothing short of hypocritical and judgmental.

We have the best news in the world, and we can't seem to deliver it successfully. Love will always be the core of our message, and until that really sinks in, I say we keep our efforts at evangelism and propaganda to ourselves.

We have so much to learn from the unconverted about how to lead with love.

"*Love covers.*" The word is **kâçâh** (pronounced *kaw-saw'*), and it means, "*to plump up, fill up the empty spaces, or protect with concealed safety.*"

We all have gaps that only love can fill. When our lives are enriched with the "stuff" of love, we can be changed deeply with lasting effects. Nothing touches us like love. Nothing reveals the God *in us* like representing love to someone else.

The number of ways to express such love is without containment. When love shows, it's almost always a surprise of some sort. Thus, the power of its appearance can be stealthy, but deeply effective.

Paula D'Arcy tells the most amazing story of her transition from Texas to California.[6] She had her Hill Country dream home for sale for about seven months as she prepared her heart for this new thing God was asking of her. Everyone in her small town knew how eager she was to get on with the new mission, but she really needed to sell her home first.

As someone who was constantly traveling for ministry purposes, she had come home for a couple of days to wash clothes and catch up on mail. She also made time to stop by to see her acupuncturist, who was in town only a couple of days a week. When she entered the waiting room, Dr. Ho (Buddhist) greeted her and asked her if she had sold her house. Paula had grown weary of the question. But he said to her, *"I think I would like to buy your house."*

She didn't think too much of it as she went in for her treatment, but when she went to pay, he asked when he might be able to see the house. Paula had been going to Dr. Ho for years. They had shared many discussions about the philosophy of life, love and what it means to really live. They had become close.

Later that evening, Dr. Ho dropped by for a walk-through of the house. After a couple of hours, he said, *"Paula, I think I will buy your house". How much money do you need in order to go and do what you believe God has asked you to do?"*

Paula explained, *"Dr. Ho, that isn't how it works here in America. I have an asking price for the house. You make an offer. I counter. You counter. We bargain. Then we make a deal."*

He asked again, *"What do you need to realize out of this transaction in order for you to go and do what you believe God has asked you to do?"*

Then to Paula's amazement he added,

"I think it is better for you to go and do what you believe you are supposed to do. My wife and I love you. That means we will do what we can to help you. Also, keep the keys. The house is yours for when you want to use it—but you

need to go."

Dr. Ho and his wife took out a third mortgage to buy a home they had no intentions of ever living in! There is no way to explain such an act other than—*Love covers!*

In The Pages

Process your thoughts about Dr. Ho's actions. Have you ever seen love manifest in this way? Is this normal behavior in mankind?

High and Dry

May 11
Proverbs 11

"He who is surety for a stranger will suffer, but one who hates being surety is secure." Proverbs 11:15, NKJV

When I travel down the rabbit hole of some of these Proverbs, I sometimes have to mumble under my breath, **"Jesus help us!"** Today is one of those times.

Other than today's text, here is what Wisdom has to say about us loaning or co-signing our money:

"My son, if you have become surety for your neighbor, have given a pledge for a stranger, if you have been snared with the words of your mouth, have been caught with the words of your mouth, do this then, my son, and deliver yourself; since you have come into the hand of your neighbor, go, humble yourself, and importune your neighbor. Give no sleep to your eyes, nor slumber to your eyelids; deliver yourself like a gazelle from the hunter's hand and like a bird from the hand of the fowler" (Proverbs 6:1-5, NASB).

"A man lacking in sense pledges and becomes guarantor in the presence of his neighbor" (Proverbs 17:18 NASB).

"Take his garment when he becomes surety for a stranger; and for foreigners, hold him in pledge" (Proverbs 20:16, NASB).

"Do not be among those who give pledges, among those who become

guarantors for debts. If you have nothing with which to pay, why should he take your bed from under you?" (Proverbs 22:26-27, NASB).

and of course this little beauty,

"Take his garment when he becomes surety for a stranger; and for an adulterous woman hold him in pledge" (Proverbs 27:13, NASB).

There is more than enough warning here to encourage a prayerful approach to signing on the dotted line.

The word for *"stranger"* is just that—*"a foreigner, an acquaintance,"* someone you might not be totally comfortable with sleeping in your home. But this whole *neighbor* thing is a bit more sensitive.

It could mean the people next door, or around the corner, but it could also include your brother, sister, in-laws . . . you know, people you really care about. That being said, we have to wrestle with whether or not we give a gift or loan our money, even in a family transaction.

The Law strictly prohibited loaning with interest in Israeli-to-Israeli transactions (Exodus 22:25; Leviticus 25:35-37). You could charge interest to a foreigner, but you couldn't skin him with usury. You had to be fair.

We probably don't need to assume that every transaction is going to go south, but it might be wise to really pray through the "what if" this thing *does* tank and we're left high and dry.

How is that going to affect the relationship? What does that do to our credit? How disruptive is that going to be to our sleep at night if we get stuck with someone else's debt?

This is the stuff Wisdom is poking at. The word *"suffer"* appears in today's text. We'd be wise to consider the possibilities of what that might mean to us, in all of its miserable possibilities.

In The Pages

What do you consider the most risky aspect of loaning someone money? Or, what about borrowing someone else's money? How much control do you have over the future? Write out your own paraphrase for today's Proverb.

Recompense

May 12
Proverbs 12

"A man will be satisfied with good by the fruit of his mouth, and the recompense of a man's hands will be rendered to him." Proverbs 12:13, NKJV

Now there is an interesting word we rarely hear: *"recompense"*. What in the fudge does that word mean?

The Hebrew is **gᵉmûwl** (pronounced *ghem-ool'*) meaning, *"treatment as in an act of good or harm."* Today's text is talking about an equitable payback—a reward for good, or punishment for evil. King Solomon's Proverbs are full of this thought:

"So they shall eat of the fruit of their own way and be satiated with their own devices" (Proverbs 1:31, NASB).

"From the fruit of a man's mouth he enjoys good, but the desire of the treacherous is violence" (Proverbs 13:2, NASB).

"A man has joy in an apt answer, and how delightful is a timely word" (Proverbs 15:23, NASB).

"With the fruit of a man's mouth his stomach will be satisfied; he will be satisfied with the product of his lips" (Proverbs 18:20, NASB).

"If you say, 'See, we did not know this,' does He not consider it who weighs the hearts? And does He not know it who keeps your soul? And will He not render to man according to his work?" (Proverbs 24:12, NASB).

Besides Solomon, several other Old Testament personalities have conveyed the same message: Elihu said, *"For He pays a man according to his work, and makes him find it according to his way"* (Job 34:11, NASB).

Isaiah said, *"Say to the righteous that it will go well with them, for they will eat the fruit of their actions. Woe to the wicked! It will go badly with him, for what he deserves will be done to him"* (Isaiah 3:10-11, NASB).

And King David said, *"And lovingkindness is Yours, O Lord, for You recompense a man according to his work"* (Psalms 62:12, NASB).

There are plenty of reasons to be cautious about our words and deeds. We should be careful about our vows, judgments, and the imposition of our ideas for selfish means.

Caution doesn't necessarily mean we should *fear*. Today's text isn't like a buzzard on a high wire. It's not that kind of message. We just need to be aware that what comes out of our mouth and our hand has a return—***literally***.

I like the fact that Solomon encourages us to speak the good fruit, the sweet refreshment of a person's heart. By speaking that kind of blessing, we actually heap a blessing back upon ourselves. Oh, how we need this truth cycled over and over in our lives!

I'm asked all the time, *"What does it mean to be a prophetic person?"* It means that you speak and live in a life element. You understand that what you say, what you do, really does push stuff around in the spirit realm. And when you push stuff around in the spirit realm, you can expect feedback. Good for good, and bad for bad.

It's that simple really. Speak life, give life, be life, and you'll get life in return!

In The Pages

Please take a minute and read Matthew 12:33-37. List five truths of revelation out of this passage. Is any of this new to you? How do you practically apply what you've read and heard today?

Fountain of Life

May 13
Proverbs 13

"The teaching of the wise is a fountain of life, so, no more drinking from death-tainted wells!" Proverbs 13:14, MSG

"For My people have committed two evils: they have forsaken Me, the fountain of living waters, to hew for themselves cisterns, broken cisterns that can hold no water." Jeremiah 2:13, NASB

Back when I was a proper denominational pastor, this Jeremiah passage was my sugar-stick text that I'd preach a week or two prior to the big REVIVAL

MEETINGS our church would host every year. We'd invite some hotshot preacher (or whoever was recommended by our Association) to come in and basically rally the troops to love Jesus more than we ever had.

If we were lucky, we would win a few souls and add to the church roll numbers. All in all, we'd overhaul ourselves, ramp up, re-dedicate, and plow into the work of doing church all over again with a renewed sense of purpose and clarity. It kind of makes me tired just thinking about it.

I love these verses, but what I'm about to explain was never a part of what I used to teach.

I like how *A Concise Dictionary of the Words in the Greek Testament and The Hebrew Bible* breaks down the word *"fountain."* In Hebrew, it's **mâqôr**, (pronounced *maw-kore´*) meaning, *"something dug, a source of water, even when naturally flowing; also of tears, blood [by euphemism of the female pudenda]; figuratively of happiness, wisdom, progeny; fountain, issue, spring, wellspring."*

Pudenda? What the fat is a pudenda?

So, I looked it up in the dictionary. It's a Latin term meaning, *the externals of a person's* (more specifically a woman's)…uh… *genitals*. In this case, I'll just use mechanical imagery.

The pudenda is only the gate, a fountain, the opening—the external expression of the deeper internal reality.

The mystery of conception, life, nutrition, maturity, and eventual expulsion happens down and through that gate, but the gate itself is not the actual origin of life. The source of life happens inside, deeper, hidden in the depths.

So when Solomon says, *"the teaching of the wise is a fountain of life,"* it's not so much about the words as it is about the heart and depths from where the wisdom was pulled.

Jeremiah was quick to point out that Jehovah was the source of the *fountain* of living waters. While the waters gush wildly at the surface, the iced coolness and pure refreshment is established in compressed wells, deep below the surface.

Beneath our passionate expressions of vital spiritual life, there is a depth that flows, spills, and satisfies our thirsty souls! It's where they (Father, Son, and Holy Spirit) reside to provide life we so desperately need.

Jesus was quick to say, *"Hey! If you got a thirst, I'm your answer! Come and drink from the deeps. The water is cool, it's clean, and it's free to you—no charge! Just ask and you can have all you want!* (John 7:37).

What a contrast from drinking the waters of death-tainted wells!

In The Pages

Have you considered that the teachings of Wisdom can bring refreshment to the dry places in your spirit? What were your expectations when you obtained this devotional guide? Has it been helpful in any way to you?

Pulling Your Head Out

May 14
Proverbs 14

"Only simpletons believe everything they're told! The prudent carefully consider their steps." Proverbs 14:15, NLT

The Office, Season Seven, "Sex Education"

Michael: Phyllis, I don't have acne. I have a cold sore. I don't even have a cold. I don't know how I got it.

Kevin: I know how you got it. [*smug expression on his face*]

Michael: How?

Kevin: Michael, come on. A cold sore is Herpes.

Michael: What? [*fear on his face*]

Pam: Wait! What you should do Michael is have a doctor take a look at it. Because we really don't know what that is.

Meredith: I know tons and tons of people who have Herpes. I have it myself. That's what it is.

Kevin: I've never seen Herpes on you.

Meredith: That's because it's on my genitals, genius.

Kevin: You have a penis?

Sometimes that is how it really happens. In a unique moment of random panic and frenzied passion, ignorance totally exposes itself in all of its unabashed glory.

It's often said, "Ignorance is bliss." Maybe it is, but only until you have to give an account for your words and actions. Then you're left with very few options. You have to either admit that you screwed up and didn't get the facts straight, or blame the problem on someone or something else. I guess you could lie, but that only makes matters worse.

If you go back to Adam and Eve in Genesis, you'll see that their ignorance and willful disobedience put them in a situation that required either ownership or blame. So, they blamed.

Eve blamed the serpent, who was only doing what devils do (interrupt our fellowship and communion with God), and Adam blamed Eve in all her irresistible charm. Both paid a horrible cost for their naïveté. A little more prudence would have definitely been helpful in their situation.

That last little paragraph is disturbing if you think about it for very long. I've often wondered how many of God's moves we've actually shut down in our own lives because we're toting someone else's paradigms for our lives, instead of our own.

Do we even have our own expressions of ministry passions that are sourced from our own heart, or are we just doing what the guy in the pulpit is telling us to do? Submission to headship (elders, leaders) is an awesome safeguard for all of us, but no mature believer is released from hearing the voice of God for the true stability of his or her own life.

We have no one to blame but ourselves if we're ignorant to what the voice of the Spirit, or the truth of scriptures, teaches us about engaging our world. We need some convictions and rooted principles for what is really important to us.

It's our life. We need some ownership. Even in marriage, partners must share what they believe God is saying for the family. Even little kids can share a role in this way. We have to start asking some questions about what we believe.

I'm not saying doubt everything. I'm just saying, ask questions. Don't be so quick to blindly succumb. Great spirituality involves asking questions, not just giving answers.

In The Pages

Are you willing to read material by authors you disagree with? What about authors with different spiritual expressions? Do you believe your church understands and holds all truth in its possession? What if you're wrong?

Job Fair?

May 15
Proverbs 15

"The eyes of the Lord are in every place, watching the evil and the good." Proverbs 15:3, NASB

"GOD doesn't miss a thing—he's alert to good and evil alike." Proverbs 15:3, MSG

It's been one of those weeks. Several of the kids we disciple were turned down for jobs they really wanted. On paper, it looked like a "no-brainer."

These smart, qualified (maybe even over-qualified), intentional, serious-minded, full-of-integrity individuals would have been tremendous assets to any organization. The interviews went great, the lists of references were more than satisfactory, and there was real passion in the hearts of the candidates. The plan was perfect, until the part where they didn't get hired.

Personally, I think the people who didn't hire them are frikk'n idiots. But, isn't that what spiritual parents are supposed to say?

As I was praying for these kids earlier this morning, today's text flamed up in my heart. Despite our disappointment and confusion, we can take comfort in knowing God doesn't miss a thing. He notices when we're disappointed.

Ah, even more than notices! He *watches*, peers into the distance and leans forward to observe what is happening in our lives. He cares. His capacity for insight and perspective can't be matched. It's an awesome thing to be known by God!

"And there is no creature hidden from His sight, but all things are open and laid bare to the eyes of Him with whom we have to do. Therefore, since we have a great high priest who has passed through the heavens, Jesus the Son of

God, let us hold fast our confession. For we do not have a high priest who cannot sympathize with our weaknesses, but One who has been tempted in all things as we are, yet without sin. Therefore let us draw near with confidence to the throne of grace, so that we may receive mercy and find grace to help in time of need" (Hebrews 4:13-16, NASB).

Let this sit on you with weight today. Whether our *place* is a proximity concern or a mental, emotional or spiritual state, *His eyes* (literally His gazing countenance) are upon you. He's got this. He's got you. He's got us!

In The Pages

Talk to Him and tell him exactly what you feel and sense in your heart today. He can handle the honesty. Does anything in this Hebrews passage touch a need in you? Describe it if you can.

The Way to the Glory Hole

May 16
Proverbs 16

"Commit your work to the Lord, and your plans will be established." Proverbs 16:3, RSV

One of my spiritual sons recently said to me, *"You have to know what you're going to do before you stick your pipe in the glory hole."* We both had a good laugh because the comment wasn't intended to be a sexual innuendo. We were talking about glassblowing.

He's been working in the craft for awhile and I was asking him about the importance of predetermined intentions in the creative process. Rarely does the glassblower stick the pipe in the furnace of liquid glass (glory hole) without a pretty good idea of what he or she wants to create.

Obviously there are hundreds of variables in that creative process, which make each piece wonderfully unique. The color of the glass, a bubble that appears, a skewed shape that forms, all kinds of fluctuations come into play.

Even the master glass blowers sometimes end up with products that are not exactly what they envisioned on the front end. About the only real guarantee you have is the intention to make your piece out of glass. The rest develops out of your skill set and maybe even a little divine help.

Let's exegete a bit and then summarize today's lesson. The Strong's Exhaustive Concordance tells us that the word for *"commit"* is **gâlal** (pronounced *gaw-lal'*), which means *"to roll, seek occasion, trust, or wallow."*

In Central Texas we'd say it this way: *"Decide and then hunker down."*

The next word is "work," **ma'ăseh** (pronounced *mah-as-eh'*) meaning, *"an action, a transaction, activity; by implication it's a product, property, an act, art, business, deed, doing labor, making things, or an occupation."* So to this point, we are to roll all of our processes of work (however you define that) over to, and towards, the Lord. That is to happen first!

Paul said, *"Whatever you do in word or deed, do all in the name of the Lord Jesus, giving thanks through Him to God the Father"* (Colossians 3:17, NASB). A few verses later, he reminds both slaves and masters that their works and priorities, regardless of their status, belong to the Lord:

"Slaves, in all things obey those who are your masters on earth, not with external service, as those who merely please men, but with sincerity of heart, fearing the Lord. Whatever you do, do your work heartily, as for the Lord rather than for men, knowing that from the Lord you will receive the reward of the inheritance. It is the Lord Christ whom you serve" (Colossians 3:22-24, NASB).

In short, Wisdom wants us to get our hearts around this idea, which is totally foreign in our culture. Give Him the intent first, dedicate up front, and then He'll help you to *establish* a plan. Yep, give Him all of it . . . including your pipe.

In The Pages

Are you more likely to *"commit your work"* to Him or to get His sign-off *after* you've already decided what you want to do? How much of this is currently incorporated in your approach? Is there a step to be added to your process? Describe it. Take a moment and read Ephesians 6:5-9. What is your bottom-line take-away?

Taunting God

May 17
Proverbs 17

"He who mocks the poor reproaches his Maker; he who is glad at calamity will not go unpunished." Proverbs 17:5, NKJV

"But Jesus said, Suffer little children, and forbid them not, to come unto me: for of such is the kingdom of heaven. And he laid his hands on them, and departed thence." Matthew 19:14-15, KJV

I love the King James translation of this passage. It almost seems like Jesus was in preference mode. He wasn't. He was in allowance mode: "[…] *for of such is the kingdom of heaven.*" His tolerance and patience were something to behold.

Anyone and everyone was invited into His presence and His heart.

The stewards of "God things" had all kinds of rules about who could and couldn't touch what in order to keep them "clean enough" to stay in the God game. When we read this passage, we usually picture little children just like our own, all dressed up for the annual Christmas play at church. In actuality, there was probably a smattering of orphans and street urchins, dirty, smelly, un-bathed, sick, probably picking their noses and rear ends—you know, the stuff kids do.

But Jesus did not reject them. He did not reject anyone.

The religious leaders were off base with what they thought Jesus was saying and with who they thought He was. For this reason, Jesus constantly found Himself having to address these crazy notions people had of what was acceptable versus unacceptable protocol.

There has probably never been another person who lived on this planet who was more misunderstood than God's Son. And our assumptions of who He is haven't gotten much better in the last 2000-plus years.

God is not ok with us dismissing the needs of the poor. It's serious! Solomon says it puts us in frontal *"reproach"* mode with the Lord. The word is **châraph** (pronounced *khaw-raf'*), and there's no sugar-coating its meaning: *"betroth, strip, taunt, blaspheme, reproach* and *unbraid."*

I don't know if we can really wrap our head around how personal the Lord takes our lack of interest in the needs of the poor and afflicted. To do nothing, to feel nothing, to ignore, might be at the very core of this *"reproach."* I think we all need to hear what He is saying to us about this and respond accordingly.

The second part of today's verse is also very disconcerting. "[...] *he who is glad at calamity will not go unpunished."* Those who declare "God's wrath," "God's judgment," and "God's righteous punishment" in the midst of catastrophe are asking for trouble. And, while I don't get to pronounce a judgment here on those who spit such venom, scripture tells us it doesn't go unnoticed in the heavenly realm.

It's highly possible that non-Christians who hear such things think, *"If God is responsible for such disaster and heartache, you can have Him. No thanks!"*

When Jesus warned us not to be *"stumbling blocks"* (Luke 17:1-4), He was also talking to close-minded modern day Bible thumpers who negatively influence the desires of men, women, and children to be included in the Kingdom!

In The Pages

What kinds of thoughts and emotions are stirred in you when you hear about disasters like the Boston Marathon bombing, school shootings, hurricane Katrina, flooding and fires in California, Haiti, AIDS in Africa, etc? Do you move to action?

Branded

May 18
Proverbs 18

"When wickedness arrives, shame's not far behind; contempt for life is contemptible." Proverbs 18:3, MSG

"When wickedness comes, so does contempt, and with shame comes disgrace." Proverbs 18:3, NIV

My first glimpse of what it means to walk in *"shame"* came from an old American Western T.V. series I remember from back in the day, when most programs were in black and white. The show was called *Branded*, starring Chuck Connors of *The Rifleman* fame.

The opening credits of each episode began with a drum roll and a formal depiction of McCord's dishonorable dismissal from the U.S. Cavalry. In dramatic fashion, his hat is pulled from his head, his epaulets torn from his uniform, and his buttons ripped off. And then the guy carrying out the punishment takes his saber and breaks it over his knee! They broke his frikk'n sword! Daaammn!

Then the bedraggled soldier is sent out of the fort, and the gates are closed behind him. To make matters worse, while all this sad pageantry is happening, the theme song is spouting:

"Branded, scorned as the one who ran.
What do you do when you're branded, and you know you're a man?
Wherever you go for the rest of your life you must prove . . .
you're a man."

I just watched it again online, so go see it for yourself. Evidently, because this guy wasn't killed with the rest of the people under his command (a Civil War skirmish or an Indian raid), everyone assumed he was a coward.

The entire series is about an innocent man's attempt to escape the shame and disgrace that has ruined his life. The program only lasted two seasons, so I guess McCord never got the issue resolved.

Although today's Proverb is steering us away from the things (i.e. *"wickedness"*) that invite shame into our life, it could be that it's not all about some terrible "thing" we did. Sometimes it is about the things we're doing... right now... today.

Some of it might be good, even seen by others as spiritually inspiring! But is there any possibility that we are neglecting ourselves the honor of earning an honest wage, doing a full day's work or owning the responsibility to take care of our own needs?

I know who reads these devotionals. It's primarily young adults who can identify with my language and personality. I've pictured X-Gens and Millennials in my mind most days as I've crafted the words that paint what I feel led to teach. I spend a great deal of my time discipling these fire breathers, and as a result, I hear lots and lots of *"God said...* [fill in the blank]."

The truth be known, some of it probably is *"God said,"* but **not ALL of it**! I know this because I've been just as guilty!

Sometimes honor comes because we sowed honorably into the most mundane things in life!

Getting a "real job," paying your bills, buying a home, providing for your wife, working a job that you hate... but affords you other necessities, changing diapers day in and day out, might actually be what really needs to happen, and a very needed *"God said."*

Those things are still **Kingdom,** and we old-timers call this maturity.

In The Pages

So your parents spent 100K on your education—are you making your own way now? No direction? No job? No idea? How long is too long to "float around in the Spirit" or chase another mission adventure? What does 2 Thessalonians 3:10 imply? How does this affect you?

Rock Fight

May 19
Proverbs 19

"Discipline your son, for in that there is hope; do not be a willing party to his death." Proverbs 19:18, NIV

"When a man has a stubborn son, a real rebel who won't do a thing his mother and father tell him, and even though they discipline him he still won't obey, his father and mother shall forcibly bring him before the leaders at the city gate and say to the city fathers, 'This son of ours is a stubborn rebel; he won't listen to a thing we say. He's a glutton and a drunk.' Then all the men of the town are to throw rocks at him until he's dead. You will have purged the evil pollution from among you. All Israel will hear what's happened and be in awe." Deuteronomy 21:18-21, MSG

There are times when I'm really, **REALLY** glad we're no longer under the Mosaic Law. This might be one of the best examples!

Can you imagine presenting your son or daughter to a religious establishment to execute a judgment for the death sentence?

"Hey boys, Leonard here can't get his shit together, so let's go ahead and take him out. Margaret and I have tried everything. We're throwin' in the towel on this boy!"

When I was a kid, I used to get into rock fights with my neighborhood buddies. I could throw pretty hard and fairly accurate. I've killed a few squirrels and birds in my day. But, we had some unspoken rules: waist and legs only! You never threw at their head. A rock in that range usually ended the fun.

Think of David's rock firing out of that sling at Goliath. Close range, right on the button, and it was nite-nite time for Goliath.

But don't picture a rock fight here. Instead, picture a young man, hands tied behind his back, being pushed off a high wall into a ditch or pit. Then the angry mob towering above would drop huge stones on the conscious or unconscious victim. Even Hollywood would have a hard time competing with this kind of brutality.

It goes without saying that, for mom and dad to find themselves in a situation such as this, something has gone terribly wrong. In fact, today's Proverb demands (imperative tense) that parents *discipline* their children.

There are several interpretations, but the Hebrew word is **yâçar** (pronounced: *yaw-sar'*), and it means, to *"chastise,"* literally *"with blows"* or figuratively *"with words;"* hence to *"instruct with external pressure."*

During those toddler years, and maybe even later, when they simply won't behave, it means, to *"whip that butt."* Any loving parent hates this part, but it's probably necessary and really important for the child's development.

There are hundreds of thousands of people out there who would argue that this is a bad philosophy. But this kind of discipline has been around a really long time. And judging by our culture now, maybe it's something that needs to be reinstalled in prayerful moderation.

OK, ok, so what if your parents beat you mercilessly, or worse, abused you? **That is NOT what I'm talking about!**

I'm talking about stewarding the growth and character of young men and women who need something more than another cookie to be motivated to behave in public and self-govern their life.

In The Pages

Do you see any justification for this kind of parental discipline? How was the discipline you received handled by your parents? Did it harm your character? Did it help?

Stolen Bread

May 20
Proverbs 20

"Stolen bread tastes sweet, but soon your mouth is full of gravel." Proverbs 20:17, MSG

"Bread obtained by falsehood is sweet to a man, but afterward his mouth will be filled with gravel." Proverbs 20:17, NASB

"When you kill a man, you steal a life. You steal his wife's right to a husband, rob his children of a father. When you tell a lie, you steal someone's right to the truth. When you cheat, you steal the right to fairness" (Khaled Hosseini, *The Kite Runner*).

I love this Proverb and the quote from this best-selling novel. I actually considered making today's devotional the shortest devotional for the entire year. It would read, **"Don't lie. It's bad!";** and that's a wrap. But there is some good stuff here, so I'll refrain from the urge to Instagram today's lesson.

The commentary in the New English Translation Bible (NET) says this reference to *"stolen bread"* is a synecdoche, more commonly known as a *"figure of speech."* We're not talking about bread that's been shoplifted from the neighborhood bakery. We're talking about deceitful gain of any kind.

In the NASB translation, we see that *falsehood* is the real culprit. The word for *"falsehood"* in the Hebrew is **sheqer** (pronounced *sheh'-ker*); it means, *"an untruth; a sham, or a lie."*

As a kid, I was taught that a liar is someone who will also steal if the opportunity avails itself. If they'll lie to you, chances are they'll have no problem stealing from you. It's the same spirit at work.

Part of the action with this word in the original language is the nonsensical suggestion that a person might lie even when a lie isn't really beneficial. They'll steal even when they have the means to acquire legally or equitably.

What the heck is that?

I can understand stealing when you're desperate, but stealing when you're bored, or when you've already got more than you need? It just doesn't make sense! It's either stupidity, or some kind of wicked spirit at work, operating freely, creating all kinds of havoc.

There are so many viable options this whole *stolen bread* imagery can be applied to, and it can be quite confusing.

You already have a hot wife, but you're going after a different woman anyway? WHY?

You are really smart, but you cheat on an exam because you didn't study? WHY?

You wore new clothes last night to the party, but today, you take them back to the store where you bought them with an "it doesn't fit" excuse? REALLY?

You lied when you filed your taxes even though you made a fair wage? WHY?

You carry a backpack around the world and then you return it to REI for a full refund? Excuse me? REI doesn't mean: Return Every Item!

You sleep with a guy you know is never-ever going to be your life mate?

WHY? WHY? WHY?

I think the bottom line here is that whatever *falsehood* we're committing (the *stolen bread*), we're ultimately stealing from ourselves. This is not how we're supposed to roll and we know it.

We are robbing ourselves of peace of mind, rest in our spirits, a sense of accomplishment, and the joy of a satisfying finish, to name just a few things. Gravel in the mouth isn't much of a finish—quite the contrary.

In The Pages

What is happening in your life right now that you realize is contrary to the standards of how you know to live your life? Can you acknowledge out loud that it's wrong? Who can you approach for some accountability?

Shallow Breath

May 21
Proverbs 21

"The acquisition of treasures by a lying tongue is a fleeting vapor, the pursuit of death." Proverbs 21:6, NASB

Dang! Are you thinking, *"Geez, Paschall, another day about lying?"* Yeah, I know... deal with it.

There is so much weight to this verse; I doubt we can sort all of the gold out of its hidden veins with just the few words we have available on this page. We know that lying for our personal advantage isn't good, right?

Our parents have (hopefully) instilled this in us from the very beginning of our life. But there was a holy fear that came over me today as I reflected on this passage.

The original language paints with more colors than we can ever imagine. *"Acquisition"* is more than accumulation, or simply having. It includes *all the processes involved in how one goes about acquiring*—wicked schemes, evil plots, inappropriate communications, and carefully thought out methods, all with the intent to get whatever it is we're after, by whatever means necessary.

It is overtly intentional and malice-laden.

The *"lying tongue"* spins, it turns, and it twists whatever it must to achieve its goal. Wisdom blatantly says that this way will birth a two-fold demon that will possess a person's life. The outcome is usually very different from the expectation.

A *"fleeting vapor"* is unique imagery. The Hebrew word for *"fleeting"* is **nâdaph** (pronounced *naw-daf'*). It means, *"to shove asunder, disperse: drive (away, to and fro), thrust down, shaken, tossed about."* If anything, it means, *"unstable* and *not a dependable source of consistency."*

The word for *"vapor"* is **hăbêl** (pronounced *hab-ale'*). It means, *"emptiness, or vanity; something transitory and unsatisfactory."* Again, we're not getting a strong picture of firm structure here.

Usually when I think of a *vapor*, I think of the strong aroma of Vick's Vapor Rub. My mom used to smear that greasy goop on me when I had the flu or Whooping Cough. Man, what a great smell! It lingered and penetrated my inflamed nasals and warmed my waterlogged lungs. But that would be the **wrong** picture for this particular verse!

This *"fleeting vapor,"* or **hăbêl,** is shallow and likened to the exhale of a sleeping newborn baby. If you could infuse the expulsion of a baby's breath with smoke, it would barely be noticeable. It's next to nothingness, which is exactly what is happening to a person's character when using this sort of plot—a *"lying tongue"* in order to acquire *"treasures."*

Most people engaged in any kind of true spiritual fervency should work hard to avoid legalism. We are used to hearing that error results in punishment or divine wrath. We easily understand that a liar probably deserves what he or she gets. But today's text says that the *ways of the liar*, the untruthful tactics used, are ultimately the *pursuit of death.* That can mean natural, spiritual, emotional—you name it.

Punishment didn't seek the liar here. The liar sought after the punishment—which ultimately leads to a form of spiritual death.

In The Pages

When was the last time you were lied to by an adult with either a false tale or hidden tactic? What happened to your respect levels for that person? Did something die inside of them or you in the process?

Plundering the Poor Soul

May 22
Proverbs 22

"Do not rob the poor because he is poor, nor oppress the afflicted at the gate; for the Lord will plead their cause, and plunder the soul of those who plunder them." Proverbs 22:22-23, NKJV

"Thus has the Lord of hosts said, 'Dispense true justice and practice kindness and compassion each to his brother; and do not oppress the widow or the orphan, the stranger or the poor; and do not devise evil in your hearts against one another.'" Zechariah 7:9-10, NASB

There is another verse in Proverbs that will keep you awake at night if you think about it for too long:

"You insult your Maker when you exploit the powerless; when you're kind to the poor, you honor God" (Proverbs 14:31, MSG).

As I've already said many times, there are some reoccurring themes in Proverbs that we need to pay attention to. This whole issue of how we handle the poor is one touchy subject!

Pastor James, the leader of the church in Jerusalem, writes a terse set of instructions to the Body of Christ everywhere! In this letter, he cautions that we not treat the rich better than we treat the poor. James had no tolerance for **selective partiality**:

*"My dear friends **don't let public opinion influence** how you live out our glorious, Christ-originated faith. If a man enters your church wearing an expensive suit, and a street person wearing rags comes in right after him, and you say to the man in the suit, "Sit here, sir; this is the best seat in the house!" and either **ignore** the street person or say, "Better sit here in the back row," haven't you **segregated** God's children and proved that you are judges who can't be trusted? Listen, dear friends. Isn't it clear by now that God operates quite differently? He chose the world's down-and-out as the kingdom's first citizens, with full rights and privileges. This kingdom is promised to anyone who loves God. And here you are **abusing** these same citizens! Isn't it the high and mighty who exploit you, who use the courts to rob you blind? Aren't they the ones who scorn the new name—"Christian"—used in your baptisms? You do well when you complete the Royal Rule of the Scriptures: "Love others as you love yourself." But if you **play up to these so-called important people**, you go against the Rule and stand convicted by it. **You can't pick and choose** in these things, specializing in keeping one or two things in God's law and ignoring others. The same God who said, "Don't commit adultery," also said, "Don't murder." If you don't commit adultery but go ahead and murder, do you think your non-adultery will cancel out your murder? No, you're a murderer, period. Talk and act like a person expecting to be judged by the Rule that sets us free. For if you refuse to act kindly, you can hardly expect to be treated kindly. Kind mercy wins over harsh judgment every time"* (James 2:1-13, MSG).

This really needs no commentary from me! So now what? Solomon says we *insult* our God when we *plunder* the poor soul (Proverbs 14:31).

In The Pages

Please read that James passage once more. How well do you think we're doing as the Body of Christ with this topic? What are *you* going to do about this in your own life? Yeah, you!

Deep Pits and Narrow Wells

May 23
Proverbs 23

"My son, give me your heart, and let your eyes observe my ways. For a harlot is a deep pit, and a seductress is a narrow well. She also lies in wait as for a victim, and increases the unfaithful among men." Proverbs 23:26-28, NKJV

The entire nation knew her as "Baby Jessica."

In October, 1987, America stood by helplessly for 58 agonizing hours as rescuers raced to free 18-month-old Jessica McClure from the well she had fallen into in her own backyard in Odessa, Texas. Since the rescuers were unsure at first, how far down she was, authorities used a simple string and rigged flashlight to determine the baby was 22 feet below the surface.

They began digging right away, but the rock was too thick. So drilling equipment showed up, and mining experts were brought in. The strategy eventually evolved to dig a parallel shaft and approach Baby Jessica from below where she was trapped. The plan worked.

The actual "hands-on" rescuers down in the shaft were a local paramedic and a police officer. Because of the way Jessica was lodged in the well casing (body upright, but one leg extended up over her head), the paramedic had to dislocate her hip in order to move her down and through the case.

The huge ordeal became a full-fledged media circus! But when we saw Baby Jessica emerge from the depths, heavily strapped to a stretcher, just those two dirty little eyes peering through the bandages and tape, it was all grown men could do to keep from weeping uncontrollably as she was whisked away to the hospital. The horrible ordeal was finally over.

Other than a scar on her forehead (where she had rubbed her head on the casing throughout the entrapment), and the amputation of a toe due to the loss of circulation on the upright leg, Jessica has absolutely no memory of that living hell! She's married now, with children, living a full and meaningful life.

Honestly this story could just as easily have gone the other way. But teamwork, new technology, and cooperation saved the day!

Obviously, the *"deep pit"* and *"narrow well"* are the images that hit my spirit today. A claustrophobic nightmare awaits all parties who stumble into such reckless liaisons today's text references.

Sure, you may beat the odds and escape such entanglements without too much collateral damage. But there is a fairly good chance that something (or someone) will have to be "dislocated" in order for you to get out of this kind of bondage. Yes, there will be limping afterwards, and quite possibly even relational amputations.

The voice of the Ancients strongly warns us to avoid the ways of seduction and infidelity. Regret and memory will not quickly be appeased. Forgiveness may come, but the scars you'll carry to your grave will never disappear.

Narrow wells and *deep pits* are damp, dark and cold. It's no place to call home.

In The Pages

Do you sense a bias in the Proverbs about who is to blame for sexual misconduct? Is there a side to blame in this day and time? What is the best strategy to maintain faithfulness in all God-honoring relationships?

Mercy!

May 24
Proverbs 24

"Do not rejoice when your enemy falls, and do not let your heart be glad when he stumbles; lest the Lord see it, and it displease Him, and He turn away His wrath from him." Proverbs 24:17-18, NASB

"Do not gloat over your brother's day, the day of his misfortune. And do not rejoice over the sons of Judah in the day of their destruction; yes, do not boast in the day of their distress. Do not enter the gate of My people in the day of their disaster. Yes, you, do not gloat over their calamity in the day of their disaster. And do not loot their wealth in the day of their disaster." Obadiah 1:12-13, NASB

If you look up the word *"gloat"* in the Thesaurus, you can understand why God has such a problem with our being involved with gloating at any level.

To *"gloat"* means to *"relish, take great pleasure, revel, rejoice, glory, exult, triumph, crow, boast, brag, be smug, congratulate oneself, preen oneself, pat oneself on the back; rub one's hands together; rub it in."*

I've heard it said that gloating means to feast our eyes upon and actually fill ourself up with the satisfaction of someone else's demise and hardship.

I will take full responsibility for what I'm about to say to you. These thoughts are my own. I haven't read anything persuading me one-way or the other. So feel free to flush them if you want.

I think this whole subject of gloating is a real problem with professing Christians. I think, on some level, we believe that whatever happens to people who do not believe like us is *deserved*. And we like it like that.

In other words, if a person chooses not to accept Jesus (which we believe is them "choosing" to go to a place called hell), we are somewhat satisfied in knowing they'll eventually see that we were right and they were wrong.

We *gloat* over our worship, we *brag* over our buildings, we *crow* over our programs, we *revel* over the revelation of our spiritual leaders, and we take *prideful* pleasure over our theology. Shoot, we gloat that we are "in THE club!" We sing our glory songs about heaven and mansions, and most of us are ready to check out of here as soon as possible.

We think: *"To hell with a lost and dying world, I'm outta here baby! You people deserve what you get!"* That's what this Proverb is getting at!

Honestly, I do NOT think this is the heart of our Heavenly Father. I don't think he wants us gloating over our goodness versus their wickedness. We shouldn't feel anything but brokenness in our spirits for anyone unfamiliar with the love of God!

There is nothing in God's retribution of justice that should make me feel victorious or proud. **ABSOLUTELY NOTHING!**

We should hit the dirt and cry for **MERCY!** For where mercy is given, mercy is received, and **WE NEED MERCY!**

God forgive us for our arrogant pride and gloating stupidity! **WE CRY FOR MERCY!**

In The Pages

Pray and cry out for mercy! For every wickedness you can think of will you pray for mercy?

Vomit Comet

May 25
Proverbs 25

"Have you found honey? Eat only what you need, that you not have it in excess and vomit it. Let your foot rarely be in your neighbor's house, or he will become weary of you and hate you." Proverbs 25:16-17, NASB

Ok, enough is enough. I've been on a mission today to find an effervescent way of talking about these two verses. It's not happening for me. There's no way to sugarcoat this one. It's just better to get on with it.

I liken it to eating ribs or a steaming pile of boiled crawfish. Just put the fork and knife down, go ahead and let the belt out a notch, and grab those suckas with your bare hands. It's going to be messy if you're doing it right. But there's just no other way to do it if you want to show some respect for the critters who gave it up for the cause!

Today is about self-control, self-governance, and a little respect for someone other than you. We hate that word, *moderation*. But most of the time, it's good counsel for us. Let me talk to you a little about the text, and then we'll look at some examples of what self-control "gone bad" looks like. It's disturbing.

Every time the word *"honey"* is used in the book of Proverbs, it refers to something that is good, sweet, and delicious. But too much of a good thing will actually make you sick.

Honey on the lips of the seductress is deadly to the naive. So again, moderation and self-control come into play here.

As far as *neighbors* go, Wisdom is saying to make yourself at home in your own home, not in your neighbor's home. Don't "wear out your welcome," or there are going to be issues.

The only way to prevent the loss of good friends and neighbors is to monitor and self-govern. It's one thing to be a 12-year-old hanging out at your best friend's house every day after school. It's quite another to be a grown man mooching off your friend's family, letting his wife wash your laundry and make you dinner.

Too much honey (honey is good) and you vomit. And not only do you vomit, but others quite possibly vomit because you vomit.

When one person throws up, it tends to trigger a gag reflex for everyone else nearby! Add the encroaching smell in a warm crowded room, and you've got a full-blown pukefest.

The Vomit Comet flies between Colorado Springs and Denver. In the summer, the heat from the ground makes the cool mountain altitudes unstable for smooth flying. If one person hurls in that tiny plane . . . well, yeah, you've got the picture.

So when you're home for the holidays or a short visit and you find yourself crashing at a friend's house, a neighbor's, or with your family, do you at least keep your space picked up and orderly? Do you offer to help out around the house? Buy some groceries or a bottle of wine? Take out the trash?

No? How old are you again?

I'm sure you're like golden honey when you first arrive, but if you're too lazy or inconsiderate to pick up after yourself, somebody's going to throw up.

Self-control, self-governance, and a little respect for others, might just be the answer to world peace. Pay attention to these kinds of details!

You may cast out devils and heal the sick, but your witness is only as good as the last impression you leave with your host.

Are those your dirty knickers on the floor? Dude! Pick those up... and go see a doctor!

In The Pages

Read about Samson's infamous honey incident in Judges 14. What conclusions are you able to draw from Samson's lack of self-governance? Do you think Samson had a clue about honor or the weight of his influence? Explain yourself.

Devilry

May 26
Proverbs 26

"For lack of wood the fire goes out, and where there is no whisperer, contention quiets down. Like charcoal to hot embers and wood to fire, so is a contentious man to kindle strife. The words of a whisperer are like dainty morsels, and they go down into the innermost parts of the body." Proverbs 26:20-22, NASB

This is just a nasty little package. The more time we spend in Proverbs, the more we begin to realize Wisdom will not hesitate to call us out on our crap. It's poetic surgery at its finest. And quite frankly, we need it (the surgery), don't we?

Most translations use the words *"gossiper"* or *"talebearer,"* instead of *"whisperer."* If you're like me, you consider the gossiper a bored person, someone who lives vicariously through other peoples' stories. The dirtier the dirt, the better the tale. The deeper the destruction, the better their own life looks.

We know how much gossip permeates our culture. It's like we're starved for the stuff. We buy gossip magazines by the gazillions (only to see the latest fashions, of course!) Pfft... right!

We do it because it feels good to know that the privileged, the beautiful, the rich and famous, all have problems too. We tear down, only to build ourselves up. It's not good.

Although my preliminary observations about the *gossiper* or *whisperer* may be intentionally narrow, a brief overview of the actual words in the original language reveals just how harmful this stuff is to us.

The Hebrew uses several different words throughout the Old Testament to describe the character of this kind of person. In today's text, *"whisperer"* is **râgan** (pronounced *raw-gan'*), and it means, *"to grumble, to be in rebellion, murmur."* Lord Jesus, help us!

Elsewhere (2 Samuel 12:19; Jeremiah 20:10; Lamentations 3:62), it means, *"to mumble a spell (as a magician), a charmer, defaming, evil report, infamy, slander, or machination (evil plot)."*

If you do the same thing with the word *gossip* in the New Testament, the Greek is no less disturbing! In one of the usages, Paul lumps *gossip* in with these slimy juggernauts:

*"For men will be lovers of self, lovers of money, boastful, arrogant, revilers, disobedient to parents, ungrateful, unholy, unloving, irreconcilable, **malicious gossips**, without self-control, brutal, haters of good, treacherous, reckless,*

conceited, lovers of pleasure rather than lovers of God, holding to a form of godliness, although they have denied its power; ***AVOID SUCH MEN AS THESE*** " (2 Timothy 3:2-5, NASB).

Strictly speaking, here are the words and ideas conveyed when *gossip* appears in the verses we just read: **diabŏlŏs** (pronounced *dee-ab'-ol-os*) meaning, "*traducer* (a liar intent on damaging another person's reputation); *Satan himself, a false accuser, devil, slanderer, a tattler*," and of course "*the whisperer.*"

Wisdom judges all evidence of this as *contentious* and the dishonorable instigation of *strife* among the brotherhood. To buy into this kind of behavior is to ingest devilry. Holy Spirit, help us!

In The Pages

What practical things do you think you could do to stop the influence of gossip and whispering in and around your home, your life, your church, or your family? How do you begin to turn a deaf ear?

Troublemaker

May 27
Proverbs 27

"He who tends a fig tree will eat its fruit, and he who looks after his master will be honored." Proverbs 27:18, NIV

"Paul and Silas then traveled through the towns of Amphipolis and Apollonia and came to Thessalonica, where there was a Jewish synagogue. As was Paul's custom, he went to the synagogue service, and for three Sabbaths in a row he used the Scriptures to reason with the people. He explained the prophecies and proved that the Messiah must suffer and rise from the dead. He said, 'This Jesus I'm telling you about is the Messiah.' Some of the Jews who listened were persuaded and joined Paul and Silas, along with many God-fearing Greek men and quite a few prominent women. But some of the Jews were jealous, so they gathered some troublemakers from the marketplace to form a mob and start a riot. They attacked the home of Jason, searching for Paul and Silas so they could drag them out to the crowd. Not finding them there, they dragged out Jason and some of the other believers instead and took them before the city council. **'Paul and Silas have caused trouble all over the**

world,' they shouted, 'and now they are here disturbing our city, too. And *Jason has welcomed them into his home. They are all guilty of treason against Caesar, for they profess allegiance to another king, named Jesus'."* Acts 17:1-8, NLT

Patti and I had the privilege of eating breakfast with some dear friends this morning. A casual conversation led to a more serious question, *"What are you asking God for?"*

We all chipped in our thoughts, but Janet produced a nugget she had been holding onto for many years. In fact, it was something she had felt stirring in her since the early 1970s. The thought was simple: *"I'm asking God to be a part of something that causes trouble."* I glanced at Patti just long enough to confirm that we were both anxious to see where this was headed.

This soft-spoken, elegant lady is the epitome of gentle reverence. She has raised three boys, her husband is a farmer who oozes steady perseverance and dedication, and she has been the satin-covered anchor that has kept them all grounded in the simple truth of God's big love. So to hear this young grandmother say that she wants to be a part of causing *trouble* is like trying to imagine Mr. Rogers as Tyler Durden in the movie *Fight Club*. It just doesn't compute.

Her explanation was juicy. The New Living Translation of this Acts passage had really impacted her years ago. Janet simply wants to serve the Lord in such a way that might cause a commotion, a disturbance—real *trouble* to the religious status quo.

This is the talk of a young radical, not a grandma who teaches in a small Jr. High School in rural Central Texas! But this is how she wants to serve her Master, and she would consider it an honor to be labeled a *"disturber"* of the so-called peace.

This prayer warrior is indeed fulfilling her deepest desire! As she intercedes faithfully on behalf of her church, her family, her city, and our nation, this dear saint creates quite a ruckus on a regular basis. *Trouble* has become her passion, and change is the *fruit* of her reward! She wants a true and real outpour of the tangible presence of God!

I say, "Yes Lord!" Amen, Amen!

In The Pages

Have you ever thought that your prayer life might be causing a ruckus? What are you doing to stir the status quo? What are the directions of your prayers for yourself and others? Do religious spirits get nervous when you're around?

Paying the Bills

May 28
Proverbs 28

"Evil men do not understand justice, but those who seek the Lord understand all things." Proverbs 28:5, NASB

"A leader who is a great oppressor lacks understanding, but he who hates unjust gain will prolong his days." Proverbs 28:16, NASB

Do you aspire to do ministry, be a missionary, pastor a church, practice as a doctor, own a restaurant, or run any other kind of business? Here is a simple question: WHY?

Let me just say that my purpose in asking isn't to squelch anyone's ambition or drive. I'm just wondering if you're being honest with yourself about why you do whatever it is you do?

I've worked in the "business world," and when you ask people why they go to jobs they hate, most of them will say, "it pays the bills." When people love their jobs, the responses are much more positive. "It pays the bills" might still be on the list, but it's nowhere near the top of the list.

In the secular world, usually what you see is what you get. But having lived and worked in ministry-type environments over half of my life has afforded me some insight. In the ministry world, what you see is NOT always what you get.

Not everyone who hollers, *"Hallelujah,"* has been touched by the Ghost. And not every church, ministry, mission organization, or para-church operation is being run and stewarded by people who are *"called,"* anointed, and gifted to spiritually pull it off. Geez, that's such a downer. But to think otherwise is naïveté!

I'm not saying I'm the exception, or the expert. I'm suggesting to you that you and I can't afford to be romantically gullible or naively blind when it comes to credibility regarding what's real in ministry and the people who run those ministries. There has got to be *some* witness of the Spirit in there somewhere!

The Apostle Paul wrote,

"And I, brethren, could not speak to you as to spiritual men, but as to men of flesh, as to infants in Christ. I gave you milk to drink, not solid food; for you were not yet able to receive it. Indeed, even now you are not yet able, for you are still fleshly. For since there is jealousy and strife among you, are you not fleshly, and are you not walking like mere men?" (1 Corinthians 3:1-3, NASB)

We need to remember that Paul is writing to people who confessed to belong to Jesus, but there was absolutely no witness of the Spirit in them. Disturbed by this, Paul confronts them on their *jealousy* and *strife*. Wishing these were only problems "back then," does not make them go away now.

Leaders who oppress others (deception and fraud), who don't relate to the people they shepherd, but who make decisions about ministry with little regard for the real "whys" of the people who follow, will have some justice issues to work out with the Lord at some point. Call it whatever you will (church, ministry, missions, outreach—whatever), it is still very much a spiritual house, a family, and not just another business model.

Leadership, headship, and authority are very much in play and responsible for the environment that holds the living containers of the Spirit. It's a big frikk'n deal.

In The Pages

How well do you know the "Spirit"-ual DNA of the leaders who feed you, cover you, or pastor you? Do they have to become something else in order to offer you personal ministry? What does that feel like? Are they spiritually consistent in all environments?

Exactions

May 29
Proverbs 29

"By justice a king gives stability to the land, but one who makes heavy exactions ruins it." Proverbs 29:4, NRSV

I love this idea that Wisdom equates *justice* with the *stability* of a nation. I distinctly recall reciting this phrase as a young boy every morning, standing behind my little desk, just before the first class of the day:

"[...] one nation, under God, indivisible, with liberty and justice for all."

When you're 7 years old, the significance of it doesn't really register, but the *stability of justice* is an unshakable truth, sewn into the fabric of our American existence. Our short history has not always reflected blind *justice* well, nor demonstrated widespread *stability* across the land, but at the core, who we are as citizens of this great land is deeply reflective of these truths.

The Hebrew word for *justice* is **mishpâṭ** (pronounced *mish-pawt'*), and it means, *"to render an honest and fair decision judicially; whether the situation is divine, personal or corporate."* The idea is that God, who is fair in His administration of law, has an expectation that his assigned leaders execute the same honesty and fairness. Paul says it plainly:

"Let every soul be subject to the governing authorities. **For there is no authority except from God**, *and the authorities that exist are appointed by God"* (Romans 13:1, NKJV).

In today's passage, we see a promise and a problem. The promise is *stability*. The problem is *heavy exactions*. Wonder what that means?

The NASB, NIV, and NLT translate the Hebrew word **tᵉrûwmâh** (pronounced *ter-oo-maw'*), as *bribes*. This suggests something more than over-taxation. Something shady is going on.

This is intentionally allowing a burden to be placed upon innocent people for another agenda, which may or may not be totally clear to them. The people are burdened for the benefit of the ruler (government or ministry)—not necessarily for the welfare of the people as a whole.

This is exactly why we have laws to regulate the influence of lobbyists in Washington. Buying votes and influencing decisions based on under-the-table negotiations are all too visible to the Lord.

Part of the whole Saul saga in ancient Israel was because Samuel's sons had loaded the country with so many *exactions* that the people were desperate and unwilling to wait any longer for a "David" to step up to the plate (1 Samuel 8:1-3). God was disgusted with such behavior:

"Certainly I am aware of your many rebellious acts and your numerous sins. You torment the innocent, you take bribes, and you deny justice to the needy at

the city gate" (Amos 5:12, NASB).

Yeesh!

On another note, ministries need the same *"fear of the Lord"* in them. It's not wise to shuffle money around to handle random needs, especially when the money was given in faith to meet certain objectives.

Helping with administrative costs is one thing. But robbing Peter to pay Paul, burdening one group to pay for another, not paying a fair wage . . . well, that's just not OK!

Big or small, justice is still justice, and He sees it. Oh yeah, He sees it all!

In The Pages

What are the attributes of stability in our country? Where do we most need work? Do you trust our government? Why or why not? Do you trust the people for whom you work? Why or why not?

Intolerably Mortified

May 30
Proverbs 30

"Under three things the earth quakes, and under four, it cannot bear up: under a slave when he becomes king, and a fool when he is satisfied with food, under an unloved woman when she gets a husband, and a maidservant when she supplants her mistress." Proverbs 30:21-23, NASB

"Three things are too much for even the earth to bear, yes, four things shake its foundations—when the janitor becomes the boss, when a fool gets rich, when a whore is voted "woman of the year," when a 'girlfriend' replaces a faithful wife." Proverbs 30:21-23, MSG

Have you ever witnessed something so absurdly wrong that all you could do was shake your head and exclaim, "THAT IS TOTALLY JACKED UP!" With just a little bit of thought, I bet you could add your own colorful promulgation.
 It's not real clear why Agur makes this particular offering concerning the undue exaltation of the unfit, but he does make it obvious that elevation of the

unprepared brings such an outcry from society that unrest actually chokes any real chance for peace. He says, *"the earth quakes [...] it cannot bear up."*

Position without character creates immeasurable damage. When authority figures aren't held accountable, innocent people get hurt. That is why the earth groans in chagrin. It's one of the ways the orphan spirit is loosened on earth.

My guess is that more orphans are created out of injustice than by plain ole natural causes. Not just orphans in the natural, but also misappropriated spiritual orphans.

Things happen, decisions are made, and suddenly people's lives are destroyed by the unfit. When unskilled, unprepared, and unconcerned leaders call the shots... people get used.

Go back and read The Message translation again. The *janitor*, the *fool*, the *whore*, and the *"other woman"* sometimes fall into roles they are not supposed to have. Yikes!

Those who witness such undue acquisition of power groan and yank their own hair out, knowing the potential for disaster. *How* they got their power isn't the issue. It's that they came into power without the foundation of *proven character*. It begs a few questions from you and I.

What are you responsible for? *Who* are you responsible for? Can you see that people are counting on your character being up to par with the level of influence you have?

It doesn't matter what your responsibilities are. Big or small, it's all sacred and weighed on the scales of justice.

Kingdom requires us to do whatever it is we do as unto the Lord and to tell the truth. To mean what we say and say what we mean.

Our servitude needs to honor the trust that any sensitive position might require from us. ORDER, not chaos, brings peace to the heart of humanity.

In The Pages

What happened in Abraham's household when Hagar forgot her place (Genesis 16:5)? How did it all turn out? This whole "son-of-the-flesh" scenario with Ishmael was due to what? See (Galatians 4:21).

True Treasure

May 31
Proverbs 31

"An excellent wife, who can find? For her worth is far above jewels." Proverbs 31:10, NASB

"A good woman is hard to find, and worth far more than diamonds." Proverbs 31:10, MSG

"The kids were camped out at the neighbor's house, so I lay in bed next to Anna. She had been in and out all day. Her breathing had become shallow. As I watched her chest slowly rise and fall, Anna gasped and gulped a bigger than usual breath. I watched and told her once more, "Babe, it's ok. You can go on home." She didn't breathe again. I got out of bed and moved to the other side and looked at the woman I had loved for so many years. She was full of faith until her last breath. She had run her race. It was over."[7]

I'm not sure I have ever swallowed down as much emotion as I did during the 15 minutes it took my friend, John, to tell his story (2011).

We were in a crowded restaurant, four of us, having dinner. But in those moments at that table it became holy and sacred space. It was the first time in the 19 months since his wife had passed that he had actually opened up to talk about it.

I felt honored, and privileged to hear this young father, who now had four kids to raise on his own, tell his friends about the death of his best girl, his friend, his lover, and sweet wife of 20 years. John poured it out for us without a tear.

My friends and I knew of the demons John had stared down. It wasn't good. A part of himself had disappeared from his natural life. It took him awhile to figure out how to go through life as half of who he once was. The counterbalance was gone. The mystical sewing had unraveled. Nothing filled the void she had left in his heart. Nothing.

I am absolutely convinced that God's biggest "I love you," to us married people, manifests through our mate's love for us!

My own wife has taught me how to give and receive love in ways I never imagined. She has brought things in my heart to the surface, which never would have come to light.

Patti has shown me a better way to be, to live, and to love. I am fully aware of the power in God's atonement for mankind, but my girl has been "Jesus with skin" for over 35 years.

I know the cross was love. I get it. I know Jesus, I know Father God, and I know the Holy Spirit, and I see and understand His great love for me in thousands of ways. But back when I didn't get *any* of those things, He loved me, took care of me, had my back, and gifted me with the love of my life.

When I see her (and I don't always see her), I understand how much God loves me. She is a gift. I've always believed I married the hottest chick on the planet. And she is! But I also carry the deep conviction I found *an excellent wife*.

"Husbands, **love your wives**, *just as Christ also loved the church and gave Himself up for her*" (Ephesians 5:25, NASB).

Guys, we need to pay more attention to the treasure He has given us. Serve more, say the words, **"I am thankful for you..."** more, be more, do more... love more.

Do it while you can. You and she both deserve it.

In The Pages

Guys... how can you do more? Wives... does your way of living generate more of his hunger for you?

You can read the full account of John's story in our recently published book: "Til Death Do Us Part." It will give you an intimate look into the best of what covenant love looks like! (Amazon, Apple, Barnes & Noble)—MDP 2018

Bad Company

June 1
Proverbs 1

"So are the ways of everyone who gains by violence; it takes away the life of its possessors." Proverbs 1:19, NASB

"When you grab all you can get, that's what happens: the more you get, the less you are." Proverbs 1:19, MSG

Patti and I are a little behind times, but we recently took a weekend (2011) and watched all three of *The Godfather* movies for the very first time. It's hard to imagine that such a lifestyle (as depicted in that series) could really be possible.

Over and over we see how *gains by violence* result in death and destruction. The overall theme of today's proverb is that bad company corrupts and destroys. Even that doesn't convey the real weight and peril of this proverb.

It sounds a little airy, like your momma scolding you about the "bad seed" you're hanging around with. But Lady Wisdom is like a nurturing protector. It will do us a lot of good to listen to her. I can hear my own mama's voice when I read this scripture.

Cops, robbers, mafia, thieves, pirates, bandits, derelicts, and street punks—can we all agree these are just a small percentage of our population? Sure, they make headlines, but they do not represent the masses. They are rogue offshoots, messed up, gone astray, and lost to another reality that isn't normal (even though it might be common).

Heavy-handed, personal, or organized crime just isn't a part of the daily lives of the majority. So how can we apply today's text to our reality? I think there is more for us to consider.

Look at these words from Jesus:

"So is the man who stores up treasure for himself, and is not rich toward God. And He said to His disciples, 'For this reason I say to you, do not worry about your life, as to what you will eat; nor for your body, as to what you will put on. For life is more than food, and the body more than clothing [...] You men of little faith! And do not seek what you will eat and what you will drink, and do not keep worrying. For all these things the nations of the world eagerly seek;

but your Father knows that you need these things. But seek His kingdom, and these things will be added to you" (Luke 12:21-31, NASB).

Here is my point: I do believe that the masses (Christian or not) are mostly emotional "smash and grabbers" when it comes to dealing with fears about our provision. Today's MSG translation says that the more we *grab* (out of our fear, insecurity, or greed), *"the less"* WE become.

We are ever decreasing because of the load we personally bear in *"taking only for ourselves."* It takes us out of giving and receiving postures because we fear we never have enough. Scarcity slides in, thus killing the grace and generosity He taught us.

Rolling along with a *"me and mine"* focus is bad company for those who are trying to *"seek first His kingdom"*!

Where is trust when we *grab*, take, or ruthlessly clutch for our stuff?

In The Pages

How often do you worry about what you have or do not have? Overall, do you have a scarcity or generous mindset? How often do you risk sacrificially by faith for another person's benefit?

Ifs

June 2
Proverbs 2

"My son, if you will receive my words and treasure my commandments within you, make your ear attentive to wisdom, incline your heart to understanding; for if you cry for discernment, lift your voice for understanding; if you seek her as silver and search for her as for hidden treasures; then you will discern the fear of the LORD and discover the knowledge of God." Proverbs 2:1-5, NASB

Three *"ifs,"* and one *"then"*: *"**If** you will receive..." "**if** you cry..."* and *"**if** you seek her as silver and search...".* It isn't a given that we do any of those. Those *"**ifs**"* give us the benefit of the doubt, but they do not necessarily endorse us. It is totally conditional.

It is after the *"ifs"* that we get the *"then."* It is a promise that we will discern the fear of the Lord and discover the knowledge available when we walk with Him. It should seem important to uncover such mysteries.

What He has created and put into motion is too much for us. It sprouts a hunger for cooperation and guidance. I want to live life well, but I also want to finish right and whole. I want to squeeze every drop of love and hope out of life's dirty dishrags. I'm not sure I can tie this all together into a nice little package, but I sense this is one of those core anchors that define the un-definable for us.

The transitions in our lives bring awakening and settled knowledge. So much happens around us where there really are no answers. Often we bark at God for demanded understanding, and all we get back is silence. I wonder if Job, after his whole ordeal of deep loss and extended pain, pinched himself to see if it was all just a terrible dream. How could he endure such a thing?

How do we endure what we endure? Job lands in discovery. He unveils what is almost too sacred to talk about. He says, *"I have heard of You by the hearing of the ear; but now my eye sees You; therefore I retract, and I repent in dust and ashes"* (Job 42:5-6, NASB).

It wasn't pretty, but Job had made it to the *"then"* part of this proverb; a real discernment and personal discovery that God was in it all. It was brutish in every facet of the word, but Job eventually found himself in an experiential reality that was priceless.

He flopped around like a big Walleye in the bottom of a canoe but eventually landed in the discerned *"fear of the Lord,"* and the *"discovered knowledge of God."*

Not facts and calculations, but relational intimacy and experiential bonding. That is why the writer of Proverbs continually personifies the text.

In The Pages

How long are you willing to ask and seek God's face for answers? What is more important to you: the answer or what you find out about God, or yourself, in the process? Can you handle God's assessments of your real motivations about what you seek from Him? What is the last thing God said to you... about you?

Baggage

June 3
Proverbs 3

"Good friend, don't forget all I've taught you; take to heart my commands. They'll help you live a long, long time; a long life lived full and well." Proverbs 3:1-2, MSG

It's not a judgment... just my personal opinion:

Church people live in too much bondage.

It's like we get grace for salvation, but after that, we do not live in the fullness of God's true freedom and liberty. We are bound by too much religion and stuff that should no longer affect us, let alone torment us.

We spend billions of dollars on professional counseling, we can't sleep, we are undeniably too sick, we can't rest, we can't calm down, and we can't stop our addictive compulsive behaviors. We are depressed, we are angry, we are afraid, we can't trust, and we're begging for someone else to just tell us how to do life.

The most likely candidate is any preacher boy with a full head of hair and a pretty smile. In all honesty, it's not working out great for those guys either. The reasons are too many to point out, but my observations suggest to me we are not living free and fully alive. Saved? Oh yeah... saved. Free? Uhhhh... not so much. –sigh-

We polish up real good for Sunday morning services, our iPods are full of worship music and sermons from the newest truth brokers, our "God talk" is stellar, and our Bible knowledge is adequate. But too much is broken in our own lives: our kids, our families, our friends—way too much.

Have we (Christians) become a culture of coping posers? Do we validate the words of the Black Crowes, *"I've got a head full of sermons and a mouth full of spiders"*?[8]

I fear our lives are too shallow, far less than what we know we're supposed to be living out.

Pay attention to what Peterson's MSG translation is saying here. **It's not about keeping rules.** Our focus should be on living a long life that is *full* of wellness and emotional health. This is why we pursue wisdom. This is why we should pay attention to how we respond to the things out there that attack our spirits.

Wisdom screams from the wells of experience, *"Hey, man! There is another way to handle life! What you are contemplating is much too costly and damaging to your personal peace and rest."* The fatigue from people carrying around their burdens is despairing and exhausting.

The baggage we drag through life's portals constantly disrupts our peace. It's like a shadow that never goes away. It stalks us and rears its ugly head when we least expect. That old dead crap is just that.

Most of our major answers are in God, but we have got to stop thinking that our religious activity fixes any of these issues. Bible study is good, but it won't fix us. Preaching is good, but it won't fix us. Sunday School is good, but it won't fix us either. We need the Spirit, we need winds of deliverance, and we need real, tangible help from the Godhead and their ministers of hope.

Wisdom is trying to help us, not control us. It all comes from a real source of love. That might be hard for us to receive, but it's the truth. He willingly moves towards us when we've got crap. God really does love us. That is why Wisdom comes so heavy sometimes. He likes us to be **"*full and well.*"**

In The Pages

Are you good with receiving "heavy" from the Lord? What happened the last time you pushed away from His table? How would God know you are thankful for His counsel and instruction throughout your life? What spiritual fruit confirms this?

Absent

June 4
Proverbs 4

"When I was a son to my father, tender and the only son in the sight of my mother, then he taught me and said to me, 'Let your heart hold fast my words; keep my commandments and live" Proverbs 4:3-4, NASB

We are at 36,000 feet, somewhere over West Africa (2010). It's really late (and I can't sleep on airplanes), so I'm thinking about the past five days we've spent with one of the squads Patti and I coach and mentor. I close my eyes, and I see their faces. In their eyes are memories of how things were just seven months ago, before any of us had met. Since then, many of them have begun the process of getting healed and set free from hurtful pasts. It is an unspeakable privilege to pour into such courageous hearts. We are the ones blessed by being with them. They motivate the teaching today. Thanks "L"-squad. XOXO

So maybe King David didn't do everything right. That family had issues, serious issues. But somehow, he still managed to sow good seeds into his son, Solomon. Despite years of drama and disappointment, Solomon still refers to those formative years as vital in his development of character and wisdom.

Maybe David was around more for Solomon than his siblings. Maybe he was more intentional, more actively involved in his discipline and development. I wonder if Absalom got the same treatment, since things went so terribly wrong for him. Whatever the role David played, Solomon describes this tender and innocent child who has held onto the royal words of his daddy.

My own children are amazing. And even though I know I've played a pivotal role in their lives, I have to give my wife most of the credit.

She was on top of me to stay engaged, keep talking to them, look at them, dial in, "come out of my cloud," enjoy them before they grow up, and fill their lives with other voices and priorities. She was right. And it all happened quickly, too quickly.

As I said earlier, we are around lots of kids. We hear their stories, and it breaks our heart. Overall, what is happening to them out there is not good.

Too many dads are just not around. Countless moms are over committed elsewhere to really nurture. Oodles of young girls have been unprotected and seriously wounded in devastating ways by the very people responsible for protecting their purity. Young men are begging for mentors, father figures, who will initiate them in legitimate ways other than war, booze, and sex.

In a recent discussion with one of my spiritual sons, he said,

"We've had to run in packs, and develop our own tribal realities, because our fathers wouldn't or couldn't initiate us. It was our own best attempt, but it hasn't worked very well."

It never does.

I seriously doubt doing another Bible Study will fix this. We parents need to really check in on our kids and stick with them through whatever process is maturing them. It's not about controlling them. I'm talking about raising them intentionally and then letting them go when the time is right.

In The Pages

So, parents, do your kids really know your heart? When they are in their '30s and '40s, what do you hope they will say about you?

Not In Your Grandma's Devo

June 5
Proverbs 5

"And strangers will be filled with your strength and your hard-earned goods will go to the house of an alien" Proverbs 5:10, NASB

So what do you think Solomon is talking about here? No, really? What do you think he is telling his young sons?

Do you think this is talk of money, power, and possessions? Let's look at the context, beginning in Proverbs 5:1-9. Now what do you think Solomon is talking about? Still not sure? Ok, read the rest of the chapter and it will all begin to make sense.

Think of something that might make your grandmother blush. None of that "birds and bees" crap, please. Non-believers would know what this is talking about. Church people have become so squeamish about sexuality that we've forgotten how much God has to say about it! I get where Jesus got that whole "blind guides" terminology!

The ancient Hebrew determined man's strength by his ability to produce offspring. Yes, wealth was a part of the equation, but what really decided a man's masculinity was his ability to reproduce or "plant seed."

Children carried spiritual DNA for blessings, lineage, and inheritance! The word for *"strength"* is **kôwach** (pronounced *ko'-akh*). According to Strong's Concordance, the word is from an unused root, meaning, *"to be firm, vigor, literally forceful."* Figuratively it means, *"capacity," "to produce."*

Dear ole dad was telling his guys when their procreative *"strength"* becomes aroused; there is only one place that legitimately welcomes that *"strength"* with true love, appropriate passion, and the fertile possibility that the consummation will be a blessing to you and your home! Too much is at stake to give your *firmness*, your seed, your heirs, your future, to someone else described as a *"stranger"*.

I've read through the Song of Solomon numerous times, and the author had no issue describing the most intimate, beautiful sexual moments between a husband and wife. He was much more free than most of the modern church. Oh, we know about it, but we're too prudish to be real about any of it.

Today's proverb is a warning that the bitter fruit for misguided sexual exploits can rob a man of resources, reputation, peace, and maybe even his health. Not only have you paid the *stranger* for the release of your *strength*, but there is a good chance you'll continue to pay for a long time afterwards.

The possibilities are too many to count, and I've counseled for too many years to believe that the wages for this kind of activity are cheap. Again, it's just not worth it!

Sexuality just may be one of the most explosive powers in our possession! We would be wise to consider the long-term effects.

(Don't worry, grandma. I didn't use the word "penis" once!)

In The Pages

So how did you do with today's devo? How important is it to talk openly with your peers, sons, and daughters about sex? How well did your parents prepare you for this topic? What was the overall message you received about sex? Good or bad?

Betty Davis Eyes

June 6
Proverbs 6

"Do not desire her beauty in your heart, nor let her capture you with her eyelids." Proverbs 6:25, NASB

Around the mid 1990s, the Lord began opening my eyes to the reality of the spirit realm and, likewise, spiritual warfare. I was the pastor of a small congregation that was full of prophetically activated individuals. I could never quite figure out if I was actually leading them or busting my butt just to keep up with them.

We were a strange mixture of powerfully anointed, yet devastatingly rejected individuals. It was a crazy place to learn the basic facets of Kingdom life, real relationships, small groups, deliverance, and the exercise of all the gifts of the Spirit.

Looking back, I'm not really sure how we ever did those eight years together. Those were some seriously anointed people following my underdeveloped leadership skills!

One of the best helps I discovered during those training years was a little book written by Francis Frangipane called *The Three Battlegrounds*. If you haven't read it, do yourself a favor and pick it up.

Frangipane's teaching on the "spirit of control"—also known as the "spirit of Jezebel"—really influenced me. My limited experience didn't totally allow me to get every principle, but I had a fairly firm grip on the basics.

The power of sexual manipulation mixed with the spirit of control is obvious in 2 Kings 9:30: *"When Jehu came to Jezreel, Jezebel heard of it, and she painted her eyes and adorned her head and looked out the window"* (NASB). Of course, Jezebel knew why Jehu had come, and her last ditch effort to avoid the inevitable was to make an attempt to *capture with her eyes* and make a sexual advance to control the situation.

If you'll read *2 Kings 9:31-33 (KJV)*, you'll see that Jehu made an appeal to the eunuchs (*sexually neutered in order to safely attend to royalty without danger of mixing blood*) to throw Jezebel down to her death. Jehu was a man on a mission. Her eyes and her control held no spell over him or the eunuchs!

It's a nasty spirit that seeks to destroy the voice of life and the prophetic. As strong as Elijah was, it put him on the couch!

Control is a horrible additive to real love, covenant, and spiritual cover! Whether we are talking about marriage and courtship, or spiritual covering by the church, a ministry, elders or mentors, there is absolutely no good place for Jezebel's tactics to manifest.

Rest assured,

THE MORE STRINGENT THE RELIGIOUS CONTROL...
(regardless of the theological expression)

THE MORE SEXUAL MANIPULATION AND PERVERSION WILL MANIFEST!

It might not be outwardly obvious, but it will be looming about. Never doubt it for a single moment. Control has dark power and will do just about whatever it takes to get what it wants.

In The Pages

Please take a moment and review Jeremiah 4:30 and Ezekiel 23:40. Is the painted eye the real problem? What is the real problem? How have you encountered the spirit of control? What was its effect on you?

In Order To Be Noticed

June 7
Proverbs 7

"My son, keep my words and treasure my commandments within you. Keep my commandments and live, and my teaching as the apple of your eye. Bind them on your fingers; write them on the tablet of your heart." Proverbs 7:1-3, NASB

"Write it out on the back of your hands; etch it on the chambers of your heart." Proverbs 7:3, MSG

Another chapter in Proverbs dedicated to the pitfalls of adultery. Wisdom begs us to not only hear and apply truth, but to allow these rubies of astute awareness to be carved "inside" the deepest caverns of our soul.

Solomon wants us to really get it, not just be robotic in our responses. We call that *"dead religion"* where I come from. It's what's inside our heart that really matters to the Lord. Here is a perfect example:

Deuteronomy 6 begins with the Shema (the celebrated confession of faith for Judaism). Verse 7 implores teaching the children the basic truths and promised benefits of following Jehovah. Then we see this little gem:

*"You shall **bind them** as a sign on your hand and they shall be as frontals on your forehead"* (Deuteronomy 6:8, NASB).

Bind what? Words.

More specifically, these words:

"Hear, O Israel! The Lord is our God, the Lord is one! You shall love the Lord your God with all your heart and with all your soul and with all your might" (Deuteronomy 6:4-5, NASB).

Zealous to please, orthodox Jewish men read and interpreted (V:8) literally and started wearing phylacteries.

A phylactery was a small leather box containing the above scripture (V:4-5). One was strapped to the forehead and another to the forearm, near the elbow. They were bound in place by leather straps and worn as a reminder (for yourself... and whoever else was looking on).

Yeah, it looked like they were wearing garage door openers between their eyebrows, but they were very serious about following instructions as best as they understood.

In Matthew 23, Jesus pretty much ripped the Pharisees a new sewer pipe because they had forgotten the whole point in all of their religious rituals. He says,

"But they [Pharisees] do all their deeds to be noticed by men; for they broaden their phylacteries and lengthen the tassels of their garments" (Matthew 23:5, NASB).

What is He talking about?

The Pharisees, in order to be *noticed by men*, had begun to widen the leather straps on their heads and arms to **attract more attention**. The whole chapter is, basically, Jesus calling them out on their hypocrisy.

> **hy.poc.ri.sy** - *"an external performance (in order to be noticed by God or man) that is void of an honest internal reality"*

As I already mentioned, it was not enough that they were keeping the law. God was interested in the motivation of their hearts concerning their relationships with Him.

Wisdom employs us to get truth deep inside of us. That we "get it," "feel it," and "know it deep in our knower." When this is reality, it overflows into everything we are and everything we hope to be.

It lies resting in our soul, like a tulip bulb in frozen tundra, then breaks forth in season with all its beauty and majesty to declare the rich hope of sanity and display the *peaceful fruit of righteousness (Hebrews 12:11)*.

In The Pages

What religious phylacteries are you wearing to draw attention to yourself *(Don't think garments here... think activity, impulses, and paradigms)*? Have you lost sight of purpose in any of your disciplines? Explain. What happens when you go deep with new truths? Describe the process.

Piles of Parts

June 8
Proverbs 8

"Take my instruction instead of silver, and knowledge rather than choice gold; for wisdom is better than jewels, and all that you may desire cannot compare with her." Proverbs 8:10-11, NRSV

Currently, I have three beautiful grandchildren and a fourth on the way (2017). Since Patti and I don't live near them, we go for visits about every six to eight weeks. Their parents are crazy people, unbelievably busy!

My daughter's husbands hold big jobs, lots of pressure, too much travel, and always striving to do their tasks with honor and blessing for the benefit of the family. So when Nana and Ba (*yes, I'm "Ba" to my grandkids*) show up, I usually get the jobs my sons-in-law haven't been able to get to yet. The tires may need to be rotated, the oil changed, maybe the crib mattress needs to be dropped a level, or the trash might need to be taken out. Whew... there is lots and lots of trash.

On our last trip to see them, two enormous boxes were delivered, sitting on pallets. I had just come in from a run so I directed the delivery guy to leave the monstrosity in the driveway. My daughter, Paige, soon appeared to sign the paperwork and then the guy gave me a pat on the arm, winked and said, *"Have fun,"* as he turned to walk back to his truck.

I glanced at my daughter as she quickly glided back into the house. Those beautiful dimples and suggestive smile said one thing: *"That ought to keep you out of trouble for a couple days."* She was absolutely right.

As I started unpacking those boxes, I found lots and lots of parts, hundreds of nuts, washers, bolts, and a set of instructions in German, French, Spanish, Chinese, and Japanese. Fortunately, the English translation helped me conquer this lookout tower, rope climb, 2 sets of swings, and a slide. It was a beast!

As long as I took the time to read and follow the guidelines, it was a piece of cake. But at times the pictures didn't make a lot of sense, so I did what all great men of mechanical genius do—**I winged it**, and then I got to undo and redo in order to get it right.

In Peterson's *Conversations edition of The Message*, he suggests that the entire collection of Proverbs might have a tendency to overwhelm a person, much like I was when I dumped all that stuff in those boxes out onto the driveway. There are 915 individual Proverbs! Fortunately, we were not left to figure them all out alone.

Today's verse reminds us how valuable each and every one of those Proverbs really is, and we're not left only to ourselves to make the application to our lives. The entire theme of Proverbs 8 is about the ancient voice of Wisdom and the role of the Holy Spirit in breaking down personal instructions for us.

But we have to treat each piece, each verse, each bolt, nut, and washer as equally important to our overall development.

Every part has something to do with the whole project! Lady Wisdom loves us and she wants us to love her back! As she says, nothing compares with *instruction*, *knowledge*, and *wisdom*!

In The Pages

So you are about halfway through the year. What are your thoughts about the lessons you've learned from Wisdom so far? How have your boredom levels been? Are you seeing new things when you read the whole chapter? How much of it fits practically with your daily affairs?

Right Turn—Wrong Turn

June 9
Proverbs 9

"Whoever is simple, let him turn in here!" As for him who lacks understanding, she says to him..." Proverbs 9:4, NKJV

"Whoever is simple, let him turn in here"; and as for him who lacks understanding, she says to him..." Proverbs 9:16, NKJV

Two different voices saying the exact same thing! To me, this is the epitome of our difficulty with religious phraseology. The words might be the same, but there is a stark difference in the character, the heart, the motive, and the intention behind what is being said.

One is leading to life. The other is leading to bondage. This is pretty much the reason why we need the voice of the Holy Spirit in our lives!

We need revelation and discernment to decipher through the coded implications. Not everyone who says *"Lord, Lord"* knows the Lord (Matthew 7:21). It's confusing out there, and quite frankly, not everyone can be (nor should they be) trusted with guiding your spiritual direction. It's a brutal lesson to learn, but necessary!

The more literal meaning of today's text is, *"As for him who lacks heart..."* The offer to *"turn in here,"* good or bad, is for the person who has lost his or her way, lost heart, lost their will and understanding of a bigger picture. The voice of Lady Wisdom appeals to the heart first (verse 4) and then promises direction to the *way of understanding,* or knowledge of what is good in life (verse 6).

The negative voice (verse 16) invites us with very similar wording but with a much different result:

"Stolen water is sweet, and bread eaten in secret is pleasant. But he does not know that the dead are there, that her guests are in the depths of hell" (Proverbs 16:17-18, NKJV).

Realistically, it's not much of an invitation. The words are right, but the motive is ALL wrong. This voice is an opportunist, hoping to profit for personal gain. It has no regard for the *heart* of the one who accepts the invitation, which ultimately leads to death.

Do you ever think about the massive resistance Jesus received from the deeply entrenched aristocracy that was operating in the land where he walked and taught? Everywhere He went, every word He spoke, every relationship he established, was under the poisoned scrutiny of religious "experts"—people who knew the form, rules and regulations, but were void of the real substance of truth.

"But Jesus answered and said to them, 'You are mistaken, not understanding the Scriptures nor the power of God'" (Matthew 22:29, NASB).

It's about our heart and how we relate to God! Over and over, Jesus challenged the lack of understanding (heart knowledge) of the blind guides. The Sadducees had lost their way, their heart, their real understanding and deeper knowledge of the very things they were teaching.

It can happen to us too, if we're not careful. Ministry isn't about programs, metrics, numbers, and money. It's still about getting people into the presence of the Lord. Oh how easily we forget!

In The Pages

So you're out there doing your "things" (can be very broad) for God. When is the last time you had a real conversation with Him about those "things?" Is He as pumped about what you're doing as you are? Are you sure? How do you know? Because you enjoy it? Is that really a suitable assurance?

Too Many Frikk'n Words!

June 10
Proverbs 10

"When words are many, transgression is not lacking, but the prudent are restrained in speech." Proverbs 10:19, NRS

"The more talk, the less truth; the wise measure their words." Proverbs 10:19, MSG

I've always been a person who has found it helpful to verbally process, but it's not absolutely necessary for me to get resolution on the stuff I'm thinking about. Once my internal knower is settled, I don't really have to say anything about it to anyone.

My problem has always been more along the lines of managing my words and ideas that are either inappropriate, or that I find funny (when they're in my head), but not so funny once they land on foreign ears. Either way, when it goes sour, it always feels like I said about ten more words than I should have, and I wonder, *"Why the hell didn't I just shut my big fat mouth?"*

Know what I mean?

There are plenty of strong warnings about tongue management in scripture. We need to take note because we can wreck a situation, relationships, trust, and personal confidence, all in about a microsecond by talking too much.

Even if there weren't ample spiritual reasons for quieting our spirits and lips, plain ole common sense says the more you talk, the more opportunity for you to get yourself in trouble.

And it's not just the talking! It can be emails, texting, twittering, and blogs. Man 'o man, do we ever have a lot to say!

No wonder social media is out of control! They gave us all our very own soapboxes!

Why do we feel the need to keep the entire world informed of our every trip to the bathroom, what we're doing, what we think, what we said, what we need, what we ate, who we saw, what we cooked, or where we've been? Really?

Who cares what you had for dinner? Who cares whether or not you cut your hair? Jesus, we need some help here.

Our lives really are NOT that frikk'n interesting are they? It's narcissism, fully manifest!

Look at me... LOOK AT MEEEEEEE!

Honestly, my biggest obstacle to overcome in writing these devos has been the argument in my own head about all the frikk'n words I've had to write in order to share my thoughts and ideas. I'm tired of listening to myself!

See? Words! Too many frikk'n *words*! It's ALL just too weird for words!

Ok, enough of that. So here are a few thoughts from the ancients about regulating our use of *words*:

"Death and life are in the power of the tongue, and those who love it will eat its fruit" (Proverbs 18:21, NASB).

"Do not be hasty in word or impulsive in thought to bring up a matter in the presence of God. For God is in heaven and you are on the earth; therefore let your words be few. For the dream comes through much effort and the voice of a fool through many words" (Ecclesiastes 5:2-3, NASB).

"He who restrains his words has knowledge, and he who has a cool spirit is a man of understanding. Even a fool, when he keeps silent, is considered wise; when he closes his lips, he is considered prudent" (Proverbs 17:27-28, NASB).

A few words well said, deeply impactful and profound! Refreshing isn't it?

In The Pages

Is talking too much a challenge for you? How do you feel in lopsided conversations where you can't get a word in? Can you get settled in your spirit without talking it out?

Pig Snot

June 11
Proverbs 11

"As a ring of gold in a swine's snout, so is a beautiful woman who lacks discretion." Proverbs 11:22, NASB

The word that begs our attention here is *"discretion"*. It literally means *"lack of taste,"* or *"inability to conduct one's affairs in a way that does not cause offense."* And the fact that Solomon attached it to imagery involving a pig (Israel had serious issues with porky pig) drives this point home with cutting abruptness!

I get the feeling you needed to bring your "A" game if you were a woman in the presence of King Solomon. One thing is for certain he could discern the difference between a woman who had *"it"* and one who did not have *"it"*.

Discretion from a beautiful woman, any woman, quite frankly is magical and leaves a lasting positive impression on whoever encounters such a thing. It really is like a priceless perfume.

It is right for women to be whom and what God created them to be. It is right for them to steward all they possess in charm, beauty, and grace. It is a magnificent thing to see a woman live in the light of God's blessing and in the fullness of His anointing.

When a woman is able to live without fear or anger, *"it"* expresses a part of the mystery of God to everyone around her. Sadly, too many women have been forced to live outside of the bounds of internal and external peace. They have had to fight for their right to protection. Or they've had to take on responsibilities they never should have had to manage, especially in the home.

I'm not talking about women's rights here. I'm talking about a woman needing to have an almost violent spirit in order to get attention, love, respect, or even just survive.

Whenever I meet a woman who has to live in that kind of aggression, it literally breaks my heart. Even if I'm on the receiving end of her wrath, it still messes with me emotionally and produces an ache and cry for peace to come into the situation. Not for me, but for her.

I think it ages her prematurely and puts sharp edges on too many of her naturally soft features. It produces everything *but* fruits of the Spirit. I sincerely do not mean to sound chauvinistic or naïve (*and if I do... I apologize*) but, I truly believe that this scripture still applies today!

I suspect feminists will feel patronized by this, but that is not my heart at all. I believe that deep inside, women know this is truth, and they all want to be known as elegant, charming, "on time," and "in season," with all the best that God offers through womanhood.

I am trying to keep from stepping in it, but lady, if you are walking wounded and cannot forgive what is behind you, it's going to cause you some problems, if it hasn't already.

Pushing, shoving, controlling, in an attempt to protect yourself while micromanaging those closest to you is what Solomon is talking about in today's text. Is this really how you want to be experienced and be known by those who are living and working in and around your swirl?

The young women of today are desperate for guidance in this arena, whether they know it or not!

In The Pages

What are we doing in our culture today that is promoting women of Godly discretion? Are we passing or failing? What evidence backs your thoughts on this topic?

The Power of Discipline

June 12
Proverbs 12

"Whoever loves discipline loves knowledge, but he who hates reproof is stupid." Proverbs 12:1, NASB

"For God has not given us a spirit of timidity, but of power and love and discipline." 2 Timothy 1:7, NASB

If you do a concordance search in the New Testament for *"discipline,"* you get quite the selection. All those definitions are important to us.

Paul reminds us that the Lord aggressively deposits a hunger and desire for discipline in Spirit-filled people. We need it! Of course, we've already talked about how it can stir negative connotations, but that isn't what God intends.

We have to be healed and mature enough to understand that discipline is mercy and love! It really does produce a great harvest in our life:

"All discipline for the moment seems not to be joyful, but sorrowful; yet to those who have been trained by it, afterwards it yields the peaceful fruit of righteousness" (Hebrews 12:11, NASB).

Whether you are dealing with *correction* nuances, *buffeting* suggestions, or the daily application of spiritual practice that feeds and build us up, it all fits nicely together if we desire growth in our relationship with the Lord.

One of my devotional mentors, Dr. J. Sidlow Baxter, taught some great lessons about the discipline of daily prayer.[9] It is a great topic with all kinds of helpful insight for beginners or seasoned veterans.

Dr. Baxter encourages the believer to pound out, day after day, sound mechanics with specific targets of concern. At first, we might feel the monotony, or even become quite bored with the process. Then, without realizing it, we discover that the breath of God is on what we are doing.

Most spiritual encounters **begin in the natural** or some simple exercise of faith. Then the Holy Spirit lands and comes alongside us to sweeten the tea. Nothing is more glorious than to realize that *HE* is with us in that moment!

If we quit because we didn't get the immediate results we were looking for, we are bound to fall away and measure "just short" of our breakthrough. Sometimes, we just have to hang in there even when it sucks.

In the arena of prayer, Dr. Baxter used to say, *"If you can whip the enemy in your prayer closet—you can also whip him in the streets!"* What a great motivation to discipline our mind and focus our heart on the things that need our attention in prayer!

Obviously, today's Proverb is about the correction aspect of discipline. So, here, take this correction:

When is the last time you really met God in your prayer time?

Like me, you probably need to slow your world down a bit, dig in, hunker down, and really listen. Honestly, I have learned that prayer can involve petition, but we need to listen more!

God doesn't need us to give him our intelligence briefing.

He really does know where we are and what is going on around us. It could be we need to shelve our daily news routine and listen some.

In The Pages

What is the last thing HE said to you? If you don't remember, it's time to get an update. Put your pen down and go to HIM. Then, lets write out some praise for our God who still talks! Hallelujah!

Wax On - Wax Off

June 13
Proverbs 13

"A wise son accepts his father's discipline, but a scoffer does not listen to rebuke." Proverbs 13:1, NASB

"I solemnly charge you in the presence of God and of Christ Jesus [...] reprove, rebuke, exhort, with great patience and instruction." 2 Timothy 4:1-2, NASB

Part of the role of a pastor (*not just the guy preaching every Sunday, but a man with a real gift and a graced anointing of a pastor*) is to bring correction to his sheep. It is the picture of a *father* bringing *discipline* and counsel to his child.

Best-case scenario, the child receives the correction because he or she has already accepted the values of wisdom and trusts the voice of authority. These are the children who know their fathers love them and want what's best for them, so they accept and apply truth to where it is most needed.

Wouldn't it be a great thing if the Body of Christ were this way? Sometimes we are, but sometimes the second part of today's Proverb miserably applies.

The odds of getting truth across to a person are always better when that person has actually asked for spiritual counseling. You can listen to their problems, make suggestions, even get a plan in place. But you can't assume everyone is ready to deal with his or her "stuff" (*and that goes for the people asking for counsel too*).

Sometimes, people just want to vent. Something or someone has hurt them, and they just need to talk about it. But they don't really want to take any *personal* responsibility for whatever role they played.

Simply speaking, you can't make another person change. Too many of us are waiting around for someone else to change before we're willing to forgive or make any life-altering corrections of our own.

I've pastored long enough to know that sheep have teeth. They will use them too, if you start pushing on something they're not ready to deal with.

Thus, I get crossways in my spirit about the word *"scoffer"*. I know it's the right word, I just don't like what it means. A *scoffer* is someone who might hold to a form of godliness, but denies the real life of what is necessary for transformation.

They *mock* truth, living to certain degrees of truth, but never really wanting to go all the way. Trying to talk to people who operate this way is exhausting! Every bit of information is like hand-to-hand combat. You bring truth, they go into their "wax on, wax off" routines to cast off every word you say.

You need a word from the Lord on how to approach these people; otherwise, they'll never hear a frikk'n word you have to say.

This is kind of what today's text is talking about. And trust me, it breaks the heart of a parent, pastor, partner, or good friend who really wants to help offer guidance. But something has to spark hunger in the person who needs the correction.

People have to get "tired" of being in control of their messed-up affairs. After all these years, I've seen that most of them do eventually get tired. But then there are those few really stubborn ones—the "energizer bunnies"—and the best you can hope for is a wall they simply cannot get around.

God will do that, if needed. I know. I've plastered myself on that wall more than once.

How easy is it to offend you? Are you willing and able to ask God for the cold, hard truth, or do you move into your Perry Mason mode of defending yourself? When you thank people for their insightful feedback, do you really mean it, or are you just painting yourself religiously mature?

Feminine Muscle

June 14
Proverbs 14

"The wise woman builds her house, but the foolish tears it down with her own hands." Proverbs 14:1, NASB

"All the people who were in the court, and the elders, said, "We are witnesses. May the LORD make the woman who is coming into your home like Rachel and Leah, both of whom built the house of Israel; and may you achieve wealth in Ephrathah and become famous in Bethlehem." Ruth 4:11, NASB

In the Old Testament culture of patriarchs, the value of a woman was contingent upon her ability to produce children, primarily sons, the carriers of seed. It was all about inheritance.

The blessing spoken over Ruth here, and the reference to Rachel and Leah *building the house of Israel*, is talking about having lots and lots of kids. In that day, all was right with the world once these gals were able to rub their swollen bellies. It was when they were unable to conceive that things would get "stressful."

Just read through Genesis. On more than one occasion, suspected barren women threw faith out the window and took matters into their own hands because they were in so much pain. I've often wondered what was going on in the mind of their husband, crawling into bed with some young servant girl trying to appease the ache in her mistress' heart. Wow! This is probably where that saying comes from,

"If mama ain't happy... ain't no one happy!"

Thus, the power of a woman focused on "building" her home, serving her family, influencing her friends, and diligent about her duties and roles as a woman.

BUT, this proverb is talking about more than just numerical expansion of family. The overall influence of women can be staggering. Their mere presence in any situation has the potential to sweeten the pot, govern the rhetoric, and influence with utmost grace.

A woman on a mission for good is a mighty force to be reckoned with!

I can't imagine what my life would look like without the influence of women. Over 35 years of marriage, two beautiful daughters, a wonderful mom, two incredible grandmothers, fabulous aunts, and countless spiritual daughters and sisters have all taught me, God knew what he was doing when he crafted and formed a woman!

The women in my life have made me want to be a better man, a good son, a consistent brother, and a close friend. I know I'm not alone in my appreciation.

This is what I think it means for a woman to *"build"* her home—her world. It has much to do with *who* she *builds*...as she *builds*!

In The Pages

Read 1 Corinthians 7:13-14. What are your thoughts concerning this kind of influence? Describe the woman who has been the biggest positive influence in your life. What is the difference between those women who *"build"* and the ones who *"tear down"*?

Wearing Ugly

June 15
Proverbs 15

"A joyful heart makes a cheerful face, but when the heart is sad, the spirit is broken." Proverbs 15:13, NASB

Joe has bagged groceries at the supermarket near our home (2010) since he graduated high school more than 20 years ago. I don't personally know him, so I can't vouch for how well he handles "out there," but from what I've seen, I have to admire his sense of strength and security.

He has a birthmark called a port-wine stain, or **naevus flammeus**, which is a vascular birthmark consisting of superficial and deep dilated capillaries in the skin which produce reddish to purplish discoloration, resembling that of port wine. Former Soviet leader Mikhail Gorbachev has the same birthmark on his forehead, though Joe's is substantially more pronounced.

The expansion of the vascular system underneath Joe's skin has increased the size of his facial features well beyond normal proportions. You would never be able to tell by any outward expression whether Joe (*his name has been changed to protect his privacy*) was happy, sad, angry—you name it. You just can't tell. You actually have to have a conversation with him to know what's going on.

I admire him for working somewhere where he engages so many people on a daily basis, because I know if it was me, good ole Mike, my vanity would probably have me working in some obscure and lonely warehouse on the midnight shift. That is more of a reflection on his strength, not my weakness.

Statistics show that three out of every 1000 kids are born with some form of this condition. I find myself asking, why Joe? I guess some questions will never be answered in our lifetime. But I also wonder how God feels about some of the things Joe must go through on a daily basis.

I am reminded of David's selection as the new King of Israel. He was just a boy when Samuel anointed him. Even David's own father questioned it. Read 1 Samuel 16:1-13 if you want the background.

We know that David was a beautiful young man without flaw, other than the fact that he was small and young. But his physical attributes had nothing to do with God choosing him as king. *"God sees not as man sees, for man looks at the outward appearance, but the Lord looks at the heart"* (1 Samuel 16:7, NASB).

It was because of his heart that God chose him as king. And it was a choice no one else would have made. Why do we always think our thoughts are God's thoughts?

BOTTOMLINE HERE: Don't get caught up in the externals.

Please steward your blessings and your beautiful good fortunes, but do NOT forget for one second that it's your character and your spiritual integrity that matter much more than physical appearance and strength.

That's a tough sell in a country obsessed with physical appearances, but it's still the truth!

In The Pages

Regarding Joe, if it were you, how well would you do with such a condition? What do you think when you see guys like Joe? What strengths do you see surface in such a personal affliction? How do they help you?

Measuring the Unseen

June 16
Proverbs 16

"All the ways of a man are clean in his own sight, but the Lord weighs the motives." Proverbs 16:2, NASB

Have you ever *really* thought about that passage of scripture? It's unnerving and bothersome. I have been around the things of God my whole life, but this simple sentence slaps me into the realization that God is not as enamored with my projections, words, and actions as I am.

He is aware and understands things about me that I'm completely ignorant to. I suspect most of us live according to our own principles and ideas, but this proverb implies that we're not as "up to speed" on our internal realities as we think we are.

What this does for me is to generate a desire to move in a little closer to the Lord, do more listening than talking, slow down a bit on forcing my agendas, and hold off on some of those absolute proclamations. It produces humility and prostration before the Lord. He really knows us. It just takes awhile for us to let that sink in deep.

Jesus reminds us constantly that Father God is all about our heart, and not at all interested in our external performances. Religious devils would be out-of-business if we really believed this. But man is slow to understand such things.

We fail to realize that what we do in the name of God may actually be more about what man wants than what God desires. That is the epitome of the religious spirit. We rarely consider the possibility, *"Hey, maybe I'm actually the problem here!"*

We assume everyone else suffers with religious attachments...but not us. But God knows the real deal, and He has already "measured" the unseen truths about what we have yet to realize about ourselves. That's what today's proverb is talking about.

Daniel 5 is a great read and an awesome reminder of how much God knows about us. Although Belshazzar had about as much discernment as a tadpole, God put on quite the display to remind all of us that he *"weighs"* the obvious and the unseen.

Verse 5 tells us that *"fingers of a man's hand emerged"* (ok, that's freaky) and began to write messages to the King on a wall. *"Then the king's face grew pale and his thoughts alarmed him, and his hip joints went slack and his knees began knocking together"* (verse 6). You can only imagine what must have been going through this poor guy's head!

And then a stone-cold reality lands, *"you have been weighed on the scales and found deficient"* (verse 27). It was what Belshazzar, Daniel, and everyone else suspected all along. There was no escaping it. The man had been disassembled and poured over by God's discerning scrutiny.

This King hadn't even attempted to satisfy or honor the Lord in any real way. What once was hidden is now obvious to everyone!

Let's view this as a reminder that God knows what's inside each and every one of us. Rotten motives can sound righteous, but that doesn't make them so.

In The Pages

Why would Wisdom point this out? Is it to frighten us or drive us to hide and cover up? Of course not! What, then? How do we respond to this obvious reality? Do you trust God with the sensitive information He knows about you? Why?

Heart of Honor

June 17
Proverbs 17

"A servant who acts wisely will rule over a son who acts shamefully, and will share in the inheritance among brothers." Proverbs 17:2, NASB

I love this verse! According to most of the commentaries I periodically consult, it wasn't all that uncommon for a servant to become an heir, especially if there were no other children in the picture. Imagine a hard-working and loyal servant who has spent his entire life taking care of his master's every need. Of course, not every household servant was given this kind of honor.

I sense something deeper in this, something that has moved the master's heart beyond simple kindness and thoughtful caretaking. This is deeper, a dynamic that has honor written all over it.

Immediately, I think of the blessing Joseph received while in Potiphar's house (Genesis 39:1-6), or Mephibosheth's servant, Ziba (2 Samuel 16:1-4). Their positions as slaves—or servants—did not deter these men from being blessed or getting their inheritance.

The simple act of doing their tasks faithfully and efficiently wouldn't have been enough for this kind of blessing. It was the character of the servant that warranted the trust of his master and favor from God. Such strong character actually pulls generosity and love out of the heart of headship.

Hmmmm... let them taters simmer in your skillet awhile!

Here's what I envision: the natural son acts out shamefully. He has not caught the heart of honor or obedience (been there, done that). When the son does obey, it's more out of legalism or duty, not love or honor for his father.

You can keep the rules and still be out of sorts with the one who made the rules... IF you do not understand the value of trust and honor.

Don't see a servant yanking the arm of a five-year-old to scold him. That would be normal activity. See the wise servant putting his arm around the 20-year-old son of a man whom he loves and serves: his master. He buys the son a beer and talks to him about the ways of respectful honor for a man they both deeply love.

Again, the slave has proven that his life is not about himself. He has taken the time to help the young man learn self-governance and how to serve the one who plans to give him all. It's that kind of person who will find himself counted when the inheritance is handed over.

There is no pretense and no false agenda. The servant has proven his love once again.

The master, his family, his possessions, and his ideas are what the servant serves with all his being. It's NOT a partial offering. He gives his all to his master's welfare.

This is why he rules. This is why the anointing is so heavy on his life.

In The Pages

How would you apply these lessons to the other brother in the story of the Prodigal Son (Luke 15:25-32)? How well did the other brother know his father? Some have suggested he was prodigal also. How would that be so?

Hard to Reach

June 18
Proverbs 18

"A brother offended is harder to be won than a strong city, and contentions are like the bars of a citadel." Proverbs 18:19, NASB

No truer words have ever been spoken! Especially when there has been enough time in the breach to build walled fortifications and bars of isolation.

The word *brother* isn't always literal, yet allows for the widest of possibilities. It's like the guy down at the biker leather shop who says, *"hey, brother,"* when I walk in. He doesn't know me from beans, but he knows I like bike stuff, and he sells bike stuff, so I guess that makes us *brothers*.

But if I were to "lift" a new leather jacket without paying for it and he found out about it, I doubt I would hear him call me *"brother"* again. He would be *offended* and I would probably find myself face to face with the shotgun he's got hidden under the counter.

Once an *offense* is in place, people get tough to handle. It's going to take some major huevos to untangle the mess. Most people are just not willing to go through the hassle, especially if they think they got hosed in the process.

If you were indeed a creep and treated someone very poorly, it's going to take time, humility, and patience on your part to make the repair. It's hard work.

Expect it to be hard.

Consider the ramifications of how you treat your *"brothers and sisters"*. It can get ugly in a heartbeat.

Back when this Proverb was first written, people handled things differently. It was tit for tat, an eye for an eye, baddest mofo wins, you hit me and I hit back harder stuff. The antidotal Jesus, who seemed to be in social contrast to every frikk'n way of their contemporary and spiritual lives, had yet to drop this little bomb about making up with an *offended* brother:

"Therefore if you bring your gift to the altar, and there remember that your brother has something against you, leave your gift there before the altar, and go your way. First be reconciled to your brother, and then come and offer your gift" (Matthew 5:23-24, NKJV).

As far as people were concerned, *brother* meant much more than a natural brother. So yeah, that was an earth-shaking revelation.

We know Jesus offered the ultimate forgiveness to everyone, but not everyone was tracking with Him. In fact, some of Israel's highest were completely *offended* by Jesus.

They hated His words, His ways, how He loved, who He loved, and His assessment of their misappropriation of spiritual duties. Take a moment and review Matthew 15:1-14. It is quite eye opening.

Jesus loved these guys but didn't give a rat's ass about the fact that they were *offended* by his thoughts or words:

Then the disciples came and said to Him, "Do You know that the Pharisees were offended when they heard this statement?" But He answered and said, "Every plant which My heavenly Father did not plant shall be uprooted. Let them alone; they are blind guides of the blind. And if a blind man guides a blind man, both will fall into a pit" (Matthew 15:12-14, NASB).

He never got to first base with any of these people!

He taught openly for everyone's benefit, but the religious legalists were so engulfed in their own power grids that they just couldn't (or wouldn't) be reconciled to the truth, no matter what Jesus did.

So again, yeah, a *"brother offended"* is hard to reach. BUT we still have to try, especially when the Spirit says we have to.

Truthfully, it doesn't always work out. But keep the faith, forgive, and stay out of defilement.

Know that God is working on the inside of the citadel also. All forts fall at some point.

In The Pages

Have you taken responsibility for the times when you were wrong? What advice do you give yourself when dealing with a hard situation? Is it working? Do you listen to yourself?

Prevailing Plans

June 19
Proverbs 19

"The human mind may devise many plans, but it is the purpose of the Lord that will be established." Proverbs 19:21, NRSV

"We humans keep brainstorming options and plans, but God's purpose prevails." Proverbs 19:21, MSG

"Many plans are in a man's heart, but the counsel of the Lord will stand." Proverbs 19:21, NASB

At times these Proverbs seem like light reading. Today would not be one of those times!

Because I've been around the block more than once, it's easier for me to read verses like today's and know deep in my knower how unshakably true these verses really are! Life experience (55-plus years, but who's counting?) has taught me a few things.

Most of you are still young enough that maybe you're not convinced yet. Maybe you still believe the world revolves around you in some way. Re-read that last sentence again. Yes, it is your life, but do you really want your entire life to be consumed by your desires and dreams? Or is it possible that there might be something more?

For those of you who have stood before the Lord and in all your nakedness and sincerity said, *"Here I am, send me, use me,"* does the Lord have his own plans regarding your life? I've seen people liberated by that question, and I've seen people paralyzed by it.

If you believe God is good and He is apt to speak confirmation or correction out of love, it allows you to move forward with your life, confident that He will let you know if you need to make a change. He may give you a dream, a prophetic word, or even an uncomfortable situation to mess up your once perfect little world. Regardless, you could change your course still believing He is for you and loves you no matter what!

People who are fearful of disappointing the Lord, or suspect He's looking for an excuse to unleash his furry on our wormlike souls, might be slower to launch into life because they can't imagine a forward direction without some sort of supernatural template from heaven or conventional wisdom from the latest or greatest spiritual director.

These are the people who get stuck because they're worried God doesn't approve of anything less than perfection from them. It's a lot of pressure, so you demand to know where that train is going, how long it's going to take, and how much it's going to cost to ride it out.

Oh yeah, this is how people get stuck!

I don't have to be right here, but life has taught me to trust my own trust in the plans of God; more often than not, He tends to reveal them to me so long as I'm moving forward with an open heart and eyes to see the needs of mankind all around me. I can't just be focused on me.

A "me-me-me" approach to life is too shallow, too constrictive, too contained, ultimately empty, and it's shrinks our story. Our lives were never intended to be just about us. Life isn't all about **my plans, my will, my way, my desires**, or **me**.

We said, "*Your* will be done," didn't we? Isn't that how we prayed?

In The Pages

How consumed do you think Jesus was with his own plans? What about the disciples? How did the rest of us end up so mixed up about this kind of stuff? What are your thoughts about how to live out God's plans for you?

Pat On The Head

June 20
Proverbs 20

"The just man walketh in his integrity: his children are blessed after him." Proverbs 20:7, KJV

"Praise the Lord! Blessed is the man who fears the Lord, who delights greatly in His commandments. His descendants will be mighty on earth; the generation of the upright will be blessed." Psalm 112:1-2, NKJV

Several different times throughout scripture we are warned of the effects of generational sin on a family (Exodus 34:5-7; Numbers 14:8). It gets a lot of deserved attention.

But we are also encouraged in knowing that the blessings in our lives have a direct impact on our children, grandchildren, and generations to follow!

"Obediently live by his rules and commands which I'm giving you today so that you'll live well and your children after you—oh, you'll live a long time in the land that God, your God, is giving you" (Deuteronomy 4:40, MSG).

What a wonderful blessing of inheritance for the child whose parents actively worship and seek the Lord! It is a fabulous verse, full of hope and destiny!

When I think about today's Proverb, I picture a parent—a man or woman who puts both feet on the ground daily and responds day-in and day-out with character. Then I see a little boy or a young woman walk into the local dime store where people pat their heads or give them a warm embrace just because of who their parents are and how much respect they have for them. The child is totally unaware of how much the person greeting them knows, but that foundation of respect was laid long ago, before that kid even showed up.

I kind of grew up like that. McGregor was a small Central Texas town; everyone knew everyone, and hot gossip twirled like a spring tornado. But, when I stopped at the corner drug store downtown for a scoop of ice cream, people were always kind to me, and I usually heard my dad or mom's name mentioned before I got out of there.

If I heard it once, I heard it a million times when I was a kid, *"Aren't you Joe's boy?" "You belong to Joe and Marcy, right?"* It still happens on a regular basis. Then I would hear, *"You must be a good boy, with parents like that."*

Most adults won't go out of their way to make small talk with a kid unless it's out of honor to the parents or guardian of that child. I didn't think much of it back then. But now, it is like sweet words of silken honey. That is something to be very thankful for!

So... what if your parents did not leave you a kind legacy? What if they were not so reputable or honorable? Or maybe your grandparents were scoundrels. What are you to do?

FIRST, we forgive and remember there are a lot of factors involved in why people make the choices they do in life. How were they raised? What cards were they dealt that they did not cope too well with? I contend that people don't wake up one day and just decide to be the world's biggest butthole.

SECOND, find what you can honor about them, and give thanks to God for that.

THIRD, begin to focus now on what kind of legacy you want to leave your own children. What would it take to warrant a smile and a warm hug when your name is mentioned?

That is the stuff that will bless anyone now and later!

In The Pages

Describe your family's reputation where you grew up? What were your parents' friends like? What does that tell you? What do you hope your family and friends will say to your kids about you when you are not around?

The Right Fight

June 21
Proverbs 21

"The exercise of justice is joy for the righteous, but is terror to the workers of iniquity." Proverbs 21:15, NASB

"We must accept finite disappointment, but never lose infinite hope." Martin Luther King, Jr.

"Jesus, knowing they were out to get him, moved on. A lot of people followed him, and he healed them all. He also cautioned them to keep it quiet, following guidelines set down by Isaiah: Look well at my hand-picked servant; I love him so much, take such delight in him. I've placed my Spirit on him; he'll decree justice to the nations. **But he won't yell, won't raise his voice; there'll be no commotion in the streets.** *He won't walk over anyone's feelings, won't push you into a corner. Before you know it, his justice will triumph; the mere sound*

of his name will signal hope, even among far-off unbelievers." Matthew 12:18-21, MSG

I love the part that says, *"But he (Messiah) won't yell, won't raise his voice; there'll be no commotion in the streets."* It feels like divine erosion in the Spirit. An unseen force that is grinding away, forging a new reality without anyone really noticing until you suddenly realize, *"Wow, we have something brand spanking new here!"*

One of the great joys of my maturing ministry years has been to watch the number of young men and women (who Patti and I disciple) that are committing themselves to various fights against injustice around the world. Whether it's their personal ministry to young girls in the bars of Phuket, helping orphans on the borders of Burma, or their relentless blogging and online production of information exposing sex trafficking in the streets of America, fearless young men and women boldly enter the fray with amazing stamina and unswerving hope!

Today's Proverb promises that the work of *exercising justice* to a very lopsided world is *joyous* for those who have a heart for the work! One can't be greedy and impulsive. It's not necessarily a stealthy work, but it could be that the most significant moves and radical advances most often go unrecognized by the masses on any single day.

Pointing the camera, telling the story, painting the picture, singing the song, touching the need, and loving the wounded are crucial parts of bringing the Kingdom of heaven to the barrenness of the earth! Solomon rightly declares that the workers of iniquity definitely feel the effects of these works of righteousness! Every day, there is a shift towards more light, more freedom, and more life.

I've often wondered if Martin Luther King, Jr. doubted if his messages were doing any good or really being heard. I mean, he must have gotten discouraged at times, but with all that conviction, all of his passion, the call of destiny drove him to lean into the hope of change every day. And because he agreed to be that spark of change, he made a difference in the world.

He knew it would be costly, but someone had to lead, be the voice, and show the way... every single day.

In The Pages

What cause of injustice has your attention? What are you doing about it? Do you find joy in the hope of an eventual change? Are you encouraged? Why or why not?

Dedicated

June 22
Proverbs 22

"Train up a child in the way he should go, even when he is old he will not depart from it." Proverbs 22:6, NASB

Everyone has an opinion about this, and it seems just about everybody has written a book on this topic too! I'm not going to hit this hard today; I just want to weigh in with a few thoughts.

Having raised two "preacher's kids" ourselves, Patti and I see the absolute value of what Wisdom is saying here, although we are hesitant to take too much credit for the way our daughters turned out.

We have seen and heard too many disaster stories where heavy-handed, controlling, religious parenting patterns actually provoked rebellion in children, especially once they were out from under the influence of the home.

We've always tried to be self-aware of how we were projecting the God factor around our kids. In spite of us, our girls are the bomb-diggity! We know how fortunate we are!

Despite their growing up while heavily involved in "church stuff," hearing way too much talk about "church crap," and seeing the weight of pastoral responsibility have its crushing effect on their parents, our girls still chose to pursue God for themselves.

We rarely forced any kind of religious activity or family type Bible Studies in our home (that's fine if you do). Instead, there was heavy horseplay, lots of laughter, and for the most part, a pretty "chilled-out" vibe in our home.

They saw their parents act like they were madly in love with each other. They also saw negative passions flare up from time to time. All in all, they grew up in a pretty stable home environment. We worked hard to give them that.

Our philosophy was to "show" our children what God looks like whenever we had opportunity. As they got older, we talked with them a lot about life choices and the consequences of making bad decisions, but we were more concerned with *"living it out,"* than with verbal teaching.

The Hebrew word for *"train"* also means *dedicate*. We did dedicate our kids (and our home) to the Lord. We wanted them to have their own experiences with the entire Godhead.

We were involved in almost every facet of their lives, and we invited them to be involved in ours. And, of course, the Lord was always invited into whatever we were doing.

Our children saw this, and as a result, this is how they sort of think now, how they relate, what they do with their own families. Lady Wisdom has been faithful to her promise. We are most thankful.

Sure, we made plenty of mistakes! PLENTY! But we learned how to repent—how to say we were wrong. And grace was always extended in every direction.

Generally, it was a great experience for all of us. The bottom-line here is that Patti and I (together) decided on what we thought was best as far as showing our kids the reality of what it means to *"seek first the kingdom"*. Then we dedicated ourselves, and our kids, to those goals.

It was not always easy, but totally worth it!

In The Pages

So you made a few mistakes raising your child (who hasn't?). Have you ever owned up to that... to your kid? Do you understand that just because something is a certain way today, it doesn't necessarily mean it will be that way forever? If your kids believe and worship differently than how you raised them, does that mean you did not do your job right? Is Wisdom promising their conformity? Is "your" way of worship the only way?

The Bigger Picture

June 23
Proverbs 23

"Don't be afraid to correct your young ones; a spanking won't kill them. A good spanking, in fact, might save them from something worse than death." Proverbs 23:13-14, MSG

"Children, obey your parents in the Lord, for this is right. 'Honor your father and mother,' which is the first commandment with promise: 'that it may be well with you and you may live long on the earth.' And you, fathers, do not provoke your children to wrath, but bring them up in the training and admonition of the Lord." Ephesians 6:1-4, NKJV

We did discipline our kids. Not because it was fun or enjoyable. I would honestly have to say that discipline back then for me had more to do with "my" simple desire for my kids to do what I asked them to do. I didn't really have to spank them. I could usually just change my tone or give them "the look," and they went running (or crying).

Their mother had a wooden spoon, used only as a last resort. Wisdom reminds us parents that there is a deeper motivation—much deeper than what I understood when I was a young father. There really are spiritual implications for why we discipline our kids.

Patti and I currently have two grandchildren (2010). "Head over heels in love" isn't even a strong enough phrase to describe the way we feel about those babies. Much like their parents, they already have strong ideas about how things need to be run around the house.

As quiet observers, we get to watch these young parents do a remarkable job in administering consistent discipline. With twins involved, sometimes it feels like herding cats; everyone is always doing their own thing all the time.

It tears at my heart whenever I see either of the twins get "disciplined," but I feel like the Lord spoke to me one day about it. He said, *"Mike, it is important for my people to respond faithfully and obediently to My voice. What you witnessed today, this is where the training for that kind of relationship starts. I am in this."*

It wasn't a huge revelation, really. But it was a reminder that Wisdom is always pointing us towards the bigger picture, a real purpose. No one enjoys the discipline of a child. If you enjoy it, you have some real issues you need to get worked out. But there is a mandate in it.

"All discipline for the moment seems not to be joyful, but sorrowful; yet to those who have been trained by it, afterwards it yields the peaceful fruit of righteousness" (Hebrews 12:11, NASB).

Again, Wisdom points us to the hope of what we have to look forward to: people who respond to the voice of the Lord with diligence and obedience!

In The Pages

Parents, have you lost sight of the purpose in the discipline of your children? What great advice can you give a young couple with a newborn? What value do you see in how you were disciplined as a child? Do you still remember the "bad" incidents? Do you have unresolved resentment? How do you suppose more healing is to come to you?

But Even If He Does Not...

June 24
Proverbs 24

"My son, eat honey, for it is good, yes, the honey from the comb is sweet to your taste; know that wisdom is thus for your soul; if you find it, then there will be a future, and your hope will not be cut off." Proverbs 24:13-14, NASB

I feel a deep stirring from today's text. Solomon is issuing a motivation for us to know with every fiber of our beings (and to the extent of our entire life experiences) that wisdom is not only *for* us, but also like an umbilical cord that ties us to a great future and a glorious hope.

That "cord" is full of all kinds of life-giving qualities that sustains and grows our faith that God is good, God is *for* us, and God loves us! That generates an expectation for the "good" of life. It's not a call to escape our realities, though painful and hard at times, but it moves us into a more receptive mode that refuses negativity and embraces the ultimate goodness of God!

I can hear this sentiment from the voice of three young men who faced great pressure and certain extinction:

"If it be so, our God whom we serve is able to deliver us from the furnace of blazing fire; and He will deliver us out of your hand, O king. But even if He does not..." (Daniel 3:17-18, NASB).

Every now and then, you run into people who really live in that kind of steadfast hope. No matter what their conditions, you are the one who gets blessed just by being in their presence.

My son-in-law's mother (Rose) tells the most wonderful stories about her (now deceased) father-in-law, who she called "Dad." Jack Egan's body was wracked with rheumatoid arthritis. The doctors put him in the top 2% worse case percentile. Although limited in his mobility and confined to a wheelchair, Dad was always upbeat and full of great joy.

His special ministry included love notes to the family. These notes were great messages of inspiration and prophetic encouragement. Most were instant keepsakes!

Rose remembers a time when Dad was in her kitchen as she was sanding the floor for a surface treatment. Dad requested that she tape sandpaper to the bottom of his shoes so he could shuffle his feet from his wheelchair and help her with her task!

Another of Rose's memories of Dad focused on lunchtime, which usually consisted of a peanut butter and jelly sandwich and a hot cup of coffee. Dad would say, *"How lucky can a man be? I'm in my beautiful daughter's house with great food and great drink! I am a blessed man!"*

At night, Rose could hear Dad praying in his room as he pleaded with God to heal his twisted body and ease his suffering. He would cry from the pain and strongly argue his complaint, but in the morning he'd bust out of his room, full of hope, full of joy, leaning into the strength of God for another day!

Everyone believed they were Dad's "favorite." You just know a man has settled on God's love when he can pass on that kind of virtue in the midst of his own personal hell!

Rose's beloved "Dad" had tapped into the deepest vats of wisdom. He realized that what he said and how he lived were a direct influence on the development of hope and faith in those who watched him live his life.

Yes, he was physically bound to a broken and crippled body, but his spirit was anchored to a certain future and a glorious hope which allowed freedom and love to flow like golden honey from the comb.

In The Pages

How is your soul health? How much health flows from your lips and your heart? List some of your hopes for your future. Can you pave your path with praise to God?

Epic Humiliation

June 25
Proverbs 25

"Do not exalt yourself in the king's presence, and do not claim a place among great men; it is better for him to say to you, "Come up here," than for him to humiliate you before a nobleman." Proverbs 25:6-7, NIV

It has the same effect as fingernails screeching a chalkboard—a piercing, gnawing pain that touches deeply embedded nerves, which cannot be soothed apart from plugging your ears. It's tortuous when you realize you've said way too much in the wrong place…at the wrong time. And every time it happens, our own fears of rejection are realized as the very thing we dread happens—someone exposes our slip-up publicly.

I've often wondered, when Peter presented his idea to Jesus to build multiple tabernacles on a mountain, did the thought ever enter his mind, *"Peter, you dumb-ass! Why did you open your mouth? Why Peter, why?"*

(Remember... this was an impulsively explosive ex-commercial fisherman. No golden halos for this guy... not yet anyway.)

Mark 9:6 reports that Peter lost himself *"because he did not know what to say, because they were greatly afraid"* (NKJV). That's kind of the whole point.

Wisdom says we all have the opportunity to develop divine and necessary relationships, but we need to be discrete and exert a finely tuned self-awareness. We can't freak out, lose control, and start running our mouths.

Engaged and charming is a great combination, but if we lose touch with what we are doing and whom we are talking with, it's pretty easy to put our foot in our mouth. It's bad enough once we realize what we've done, but it's just plain humiliating when someone else has to remind us of our place.

Jesus was never rude, but his questions had the potential to dismantle and expose people's religious ambition. For example:

"Then the mother of the sons of Zebedee came to Jesus with her sons, bowing down and making a request of Him. And He said to her, 'What do you wish?' She said to Him, 'Command that in Your kingdom these two sons of mine may sit one on Your right and one on Your left.' But Jesus answered, 'You do not know what you are asking. [gulp] *Are you able to drink the cup that I am about*

to drink?'"

[gulp, gulp]

"They said to Him, 'We are able.'"

Geez guys, really? Are you sure? Is your mouth running because you're nervous? Are you really that ambitious, or do you just not have a clue? That is some scary business, gentlemen!

"He said to them, 'My cup you shall drink; but to sit on My right and on My left, this is not Mine to give, but it is for those for whom it has been prepared by My Father'" (Matthew 20:20-23, NASB).

They eventually did drink from the cup, but they obviously didn't know what they were talking about. If your "lead-in" is all about your wants and involves an unwarranted summary of your credentials, you've already hosed yourself. By the time you realize your mistake... it's too late.

A concerted effort of courtesy and respectful honor of someone else, before your own validation, is always the sure move in any situation, especially in the presence of someone to whom honor is due.

In The Pages

How quick are you to validate yourself before you're even asked about your life? How well do you listen to others? When you encounter a person suffering from the "Me-Monster," how does it affect you? What are the traits of the "Me-Monster?" Read Matthew 23:11-12. How does these verses apply to today's topic?

Recycled Dog Puke

June 26
Proverbs 26

"As a dog eats its own vomit, so fools recycle silliness." Proverbs 26:11, MSG

Sorry about the imagery, but I didn't write it. I find it interesting that Peter referenced this same proverb to front out false teachers:

"They prove the truth of this proverb: "A dog returns to its vomit." And

another says, "A washed pig returns to the mud." (2 Peter 2:22, NLT). Take a moment and read the whole chapter... it's brutal!

There had been a long string of offenses, and the Apostle was addressing these false teachers rather harshly, because they knew better. They had been exposed to the truth and had still returned to their old natures and worldly ideals like *"a dog goes back to its own vomit"* and *"a scrubbed-up pig heads for the mud."*

These guys were selfish, conceited, and prone to exploit the people for their own benefit. If they wanted to live in their own little commune of heresy, fine, go for it. But they had found a way to infiltrate the church and spread their indoctrinate cancer.

Peter was undone and fed up about the whole thing and had exploded in disgust and indignation. Thus, Peter concludes the chapter with about the most offensive effigy he could reference.

I love Peterson's words today, *"so fools recycle silliness."* To recycle something means to convert a dead or used object into something we can use again.

Romans 6:1-4 says our old nature is dead. And it remains dead unless we resurrect that old nature. We do NOT have to respond to the temptations of the flesh. We do NOT have to recycle sin.

In fact, a dead man cannot sin. Romans 6:3 says, *"we were baptized into His death"* (NASB). I don't think we really get this. If we did, it would solve a lot of our issues.

It seems we have just accepted the fact that we are going to sin, and when we do sin, grace will take care of it. Of course grace IS amazing, but we need a conscious, predetermined constitution that we do not have to answer sin when it calls.

Why? Because we were baptized into the death of Christ!

We do not have to lie. We do not have to fool around sexually. We do not have to abuse, reject, and wound. We do not have to harbor unforgiveness and carry a bitter spirit. We do not have to do any of those things!

I would not be so bold as to proclaim anyone's purity because of some external behavior, but we can stop the recycling of old habits and old worldly pacifiers that feed our petty needs for self-indulgence and fleshly comfort. The personal, spiritual "vacation" from responsibility and "right living" never works out well for any of us.

Why? Because we still have too much of "ME" in the mix.

Even if someone does wound or lash out at us, we still need to evaluate the "why" of that process. Maybe they were just having a rotten day. Little happens in our life that justifies the recycling of our moral silliness.

There was more value in His death on the cross than just our reservation in heaven.

In The Pages

Do you expect to sin? How much thought have you given to the concept that you do not have to sin? Take a moment to journal your thoughts concerning the cycle of sin in your own life. What needs to be addressed in your heart that poses a big challenge to your inner peace and external rest?

Discerning Authority

June 27
Proverbs 27

"Let another praise you, and not your own mouth; a stranger, and not your own lips." Proverbs 27:2, NASB

Nothing is quicker to throw the sheets back on our own insecurities than when we open our mouths to sing our own praises. Of course, it's alright to affirm ourselves when a good work has been accomplished, but that's not what Wisdom is talking about here.

This has more to do with our vain attempts to impress others in order to be accepted, liked, or welcomed into whatever we are trying to get into. Honest assessments of our skills and abilities are necessary at times.

We need to be able to articulate what we can do when we're in a job interview. But that deeper need to sway public opinion so I feel good about "me" just has an all-around bad odor to it. People can smell it before the wrapper is even off.

It usually makes me feel sad to be around people who can't help themselves when it comes to self-praise. I can only assume they're not getting the kind of affirmation they really need, so they take matters into their own hands.

Paul was having issues in the church in Corinth. Despite all the teaching he had done and all the time he had spent with the saints, some were questioning Paul's authority as an apostle and had begun to gravitate to other teachers. Paul addresses the issue in 2 Corinthians 10.

Because this church knew Paul and understood he had other missionary endeavors, he felt the need to remind them of the authority he had, even while absent. Though he was ministering elsewhere, his authority was still in place.

Paul was not one to boast. But for the benefit of the entire body and because his authority was being challenged by outsiders, Paul had to flex a little muscle in order to enforce his authority and remind the young church that he was indeed "apostle" by God's design. He summarizes beautifully,

"But HE WHO BOASTS IS TO BOAST IN THE LORD. For it is not he who commends himself that is approved, but he whom the Lord commends" (2 Corinthians 10:17-18, NASB).

This was not the ego trip of an insecure and wounded young man—just a simple reminder that nothing had changed in the spiritual realm and they were still under his authority. It is an awesome reminder for all of us in considering proper protocols with our leaders in ministry.

Each of us still has a responsibility to discern each leader's "life juice" and examine the fruit produced, even when that leader is not in our immediate proximity. There is a huge difference between reminding a person, or a "church," of one's authority, and ceaseless name-dropping and bragging in order to leverage respect, honor, and trust. That doesn't work with mature people.

Rightfully so!

In The Pages

When was the last time you heard an individual attempt to convince you with words why you should trust them? Did they persuade you? What happens to you when another person's "me monster" manifests during a dialogue? Can you hang with them, or do you start looking for exits?

NOT Good!

June 28
Proverbs 28

"To show partiality is not good, because for a piece of bread a man will transgress." Proverbs 28:21, NKJV

"Playing favorites is always a bad thing; you can do great harm in seemingly harmless ways." Proverbs 28:21, MSG

The Hebrew word for *"partiality"* tells us quite a bit about the person being described here. It literally means, *"regards the face."* So basically, we have some sort of decision being made for very superficial reasons—prejudice, profiling, discrimination, chauvinism, bias, narrow-mindedness, sexism, bigotry, or insensitive preconceptions.

Whatever the reason, the miscarriage of justice has tipped the scales of preference unfairly. Wisdom warns us more than once that God does not tolerate this kind of injustice. See for yourself:

"To show partiality to the wicked is not good, Nor to thrust aside the righteous in judgment" (Proverbs 18:5, NASB).

And then there is this little beauty,

"These also are sayings of the wise. To show partiality in judgment is not good" (Proverbs 23:24, NASB).

Plainly, this is NOT good.

The second part of this verse may mean different things to different people. It's up to us to apply the warning to our own lives.

Any person shallow enough to discriminate for any reason can also be easily bought, even when it comes to the most meager and simple things. In other words, a person who has already "tipped the scales" unjustly doesn't need much convincing to do anything else. They're already corrupt. Even *a piece of bread* is enough of a bribe to entice their inequity. It's a pathetic picture of emptiness.

What's even more disturbing here is that *partiality* causes desperate people to take matters into their own hands in efforts to avoid their own demise. If a man can't get bread to feed his family because of some sort of injustice, you can pretty much expect that man to move to desperate measures or witness the breaking of his spirit altogether.

Again... it is NOT good.

Sadly, I do see this in family systems from time to time. Where people are loved but not necessarily favored unless they play by the rules of the system.

Grown kids who conform and mold to the demands of their parents find themselves the benefactors of tremendous favor, whereas kids who aren't as compliant or gifted might be totally overlooked. Common or not, it does happen.

As parents, we have to be careful with this. So that one kid has a special talent or is naturally gifted. What do you see and appreciate about the other kid(s)? The key is real and honest appreciation for everyone involved.

Diversity is good, and it was God's idea in the first place! But when the corruptive lust of *partiality* is permitted to exist, people do what's necessary to "level the playing fields," and uprisings happen.

Sometimes it looks like rebellion; other times it looks like revolution. Guess it depends on your perspective. But sooner or later, the injustice of *partiality* will be removed from power, and equity will reign.

In The Pages

Have you ever benefited from partiality and privilege? Looking back, how do you feel about that now? If you benefited, was it at the expense of someone else? How do you think they look back on that experience?

Losing Focus

June 29
Proverbs 29

"Where there is no vision, the people perish: but he that keepeth the law, happy is he." Proverbs 29:18, KJV

"Where there is no vision, the people are unrestrained, but happy is he that keeps the law." Proverbs, 29:18, NASB

A friend of mine, the young pastor of a vibrant church on the Canadian border, told me a chilling tale over drinks and a cigar one night. The color had left Mark's face. His eyes were glazed and steely. Then, like a backhoe overloaded with manure, he tipped the bucket and dropped his load right in the middle of our man time.

"I kid you not, this all happened within 12 months of my dad leaving our home. He never even said he was leaving...he just kind of disappeared."

Ugh... but there was more...

"By age 17, my oldest brother was diagnosed as an alcoholic. My sister, also 17, started dancing in a strip club. I was 16 and had lost my virginity. My little brother was in juvenile detention by age nine. And my youngest brother has battled depression ever since Dad left. One year, Mike! That all happened within one year."

All I could do was sip and choke it back. Then he said something I'll never forget:

"Dad lost vision. The one who had the responsibility for all of us turned inward, became consumed with himself, and the rest of us were left to fend for ourselves."

Like a howling dog, this tale barks *"unrestrained."* **Dad lost vision.** Like an endless repeat on an old 8 track, I just kept hearing it in my mind, over and over and over. In that fresh mound of fertilizer, there it was, in all of its tragically pathetic reality...

Dad lost vision.

Men who lose their focus get bored. When men turn inward to satisfy "self" above everything else in their lives, they do immeasurable damage.

Headship is spiritual, whether a man ever realizes that or not. But it's also very practical and tediously real. I tell young men constantly, whenever you throw down and demand that you be satisfied first and foremost, someone else always gets wounded at your expense.

Whenever you take something for yourself that is not yours to take, or is inappropriate, you sow a spirit of rejection that does immense damage to what follows behind.

Maybe I'm naïve, but what I consider to be part of the responsibility of being a man is to willingly sacrifice so that everyone else gets what they need...

FIRST.

Trust me... it pays huge dividends in marriage and in family for the "man" to make honorable calls about such things. Too many guys think they fulfill their spiritual duties by going to church on Sunday. It can't hurt, but in no way does that guarantee the man is honorably leading his family.

It is so important for men to understand these concepts. Lose your focus for a moment, and the bonds of trusting protection lose their grip. And you do realize "who" is waiting nearby to pick up the fallen pieces?

In The Pages

See Exodus 34:6-7. What do you think these verses are suggesting about the effects of our bad choices upon our children and the generations after us? So Dad left you, divorced your mom, checked out early, abused you, and took what was not his to take. Are you still carrying that baggage, or have you found a way to forgive and get your healing?

Unwashed

June 30
Proverbs 30

"There is a kind who is pure in his own eyes, yet is not washed from his filthiness." Proverbs 30:12, NASB

"There is a generation that is pure in its own eyes, yet is not washed from its filthiness." Proverbs 30:12, NKJV

It would be totally unjust to just do a "flyby" on this verse without really giving it some prayerful thought. Agur mentions four different kinds of "undesirables" here: those *disrespectful of authority* (verse 11), *hypocrites* (verse 12), the *arrogant* (verse 13), and the *slayers of the innocent* (verse 14).

The Keil & Delitzsch Commentary summarizes this undesirable group as *"the blackest ingratitude, loathsome self-righteousness, arrogant presumption, and unmerciful covetousness."* While each of these is shamefully accurate, and equally offensive, the one we're talking about today (*hypocrites*) might be the most troubling spiritually.

"All the ways of a man are clean in his own sight, but the Lord weighs the motives" (Proverbs 16:2, NASB).

How are we to deal with such a penetrating truth?

The fact that we can spot hypocrisy a mile away isn't saying that much. Hypocrisy is everywhere, and the people who wear it usually like it big and gaudy.

So you seeing hypocrisy in me is like child's play, and me seeing it in you is a piece of cake, but what about us seeing the crap in our own heart? That is a little tougher and much more difficult to deal with.

It takes a certain kind of individual to even remotely suspect his or her own hypocrisy, and we rarely do.

Why?

It could be that our pride, prejudices, and emotional blind spots prevent us from knowing the real motives of our heart. Or it could be that we're conditioned to believe that cleanliness and purity of heart happens via external works. Maybe we think that righteousness, or sanctification, can be merited because of our action and our right thoughts.

NEWSFLASH:
None of these things have anything to do with having a clean heart.

"The Pharisee stood and was praying this to himself: 'God, I thank You that I am not like other people: swindlers, unjust, adulterers, or even like this tax collector. 'I fast twice a week; I pay tithes of all that I get.' "But the tax collector, standing some distance away, was even unwilling to lift up his eyes to heaven, but was beating his breast, saying, 'God, be merciful to me, the sinner!' "I tell you, this man went to his house justified rather than the other; for everyone who exalts himself will be humbled, but he who humbles himself will be exalted" Luke 18:11-14, (NASB).

See, even the most rabid pursuers of righteousness failed miserably in the eyes of the Lord. Jesus links authentic humility to the real stuff, and that creates a problem for people who are proud and petrified in their own belief systems.

For whatever it's worth to you, I don't think the ones we deem as *lost* are the ones automatically at risk for being guilty of today's Wisdom lesson. I think it is *us*, the ones who actually know some truth about the Lord.

We've either forgotten, or no longer care, that dead religion is as the *filthiness* of idolatry. We have traded our sensitive seeking hearts for arrogantly settled theological positions and pride in our spiritual communities.

I'm not sure how that is any different from those Pharisee guys Jesus confronted on a regular basis.

In The Pages

Do you trust all the motives in your heart for purity? Do you have someone in your life that will call "bullshit" on your pretense and spiritual arrogance when they see it manifest? When was the last time you repented for your religious appetites and spirit numbing ruts of thought?

The word "Christian" begins with the word "Christ." How much of his personality is evident in your world vision and how you treat people? If all you can do is judge others for how wrong they are compared to how right you are... you might want to consider removing the word "Christian" from your resume. Jesus chose people over theology every time. —MDP 2018

ENDNOTES

April 7 – [1]I've known Isaiah and Carol Reed for a long time. They're the real deal. You can find them on the internet pretty easy. Isaiah is pure evangelist. He cares about one thing: souls! If you contact him, you need to know that up front.

April 17 – [2]J. T. Lyonette surrendered his battle with pancreatic cancer on July 9, 2012. He was 51 years old. J. T. was loved well by his wife Michelle and two daughters (Nikki and Corrine). Many friends and family miss him dearly.

May 7 – [3]Mary Alice Dueger (Dec 2, 1913 – Dec 6, 2009). Such an elegant lady. Classy through and through. We miss her very much.

May 8 – [4]I received my Masters of Divinity from Southwestern Baptist Theological Seminary in Ft. Worth, Tx.

[5]The sermon title was: *The Creation: Chance or Choice?* by Dr. Bill Tolar. Dr. Tolar was highly respected on campus. A brilliant man.

May 10 – [6]*A Spirituality For The Two Halves of Life* with Father Richard Rohr and Paula D'Arcy (2004—6 CDs). St. Anthony Messenger Press. Used by permission.

May 31 – [7]Anna Laurie Plummer Rambeau (October 27, 1964 – August 6, 2009). Her husband John is the Sr. Pastor of High Point Church, Waco, Tx. John is a true pastor and a real blessing to his family and friends. Hearing John tell the story of his beloved Anna wrecked me for days! I'm grateful I was present to hear such a thing.

June 3 – [8]That lyric is from the song *Hotel Illness* by Rich Robinson, Chris Robinson © Warner/Chappell Music, Inc. Used by permission.

June 12 – [9]The first devotional I ever owned was written by Dr. J. Sidlow Baxter, *Awake, My Heart!* Millions of copies have been sold of this devotional. Dr Baxter was the personal mentor to Dr. H. D. McCarty, the man who baptized me while a student at the University of Arkansas in 1978. I heard Dr. Baxter preach numerous times. I was always captivated by Brother Sid's anointing and tender spirit.

RESOURCES

BIBLE KEY:

KJV - *The Holy Bible, King James Version* (Public Domain).

MSG – Peterson, E. H. (2005). *The Message: the Bible in contemporary language.* Colorado Springs, CO: NavPress. Used by permission.

NASB - *New American Standard Bible: 1995 update.* (1995). LaHabra, CA: The Lockman Foundation. Used by permission.

LXX - Brenton, L. C. L. (1870). *The Septuagint Version of the Old Testament: English Translation.* London: Samuel Bagster and Sons.

NCV - *The Everyday Bible: New Century Version.* (2005). Nashville, TN: Thomas Nelson, Inc. Used by permission.

NET - Biblical Studies Press. (2006). *The NET Bible First Edition; Bible. English. NET Bible.; The NET Bible.* Biblical Studies Press. Used by permission.

NIV – *THE HOLY BIBLE, NEW INTERNATIONAL VERSION®.* Copyright © 1973, 1978, 1984 by International Bible Society. Used by permission.

NKJV - *The New King James Version.* (1982). Nashville: Thomas Nelson. Used by permission.

NLT - *New Living Translation* (1996, 2005, 2007). Tyndale House Publishers, Inc., Carol Stream, Illinois 60188. Used by permission.

NRSV - *The Holy Bible: New Revised Standard Version.* (1989). Nashville: Thomas Nelson Publishers. Used by permission.

RSV - *Revised Standard Version of the Bible*, copyright 1952 [2nd edition, 1971] by the Division of Christian Education of the National Council of the Churches of Christ in the United States of America. Used by permission.

TLB – *The Living Bible* (1971) Tyndale House Publishers, Inc., Wheaton, IL 60189. Used by permission.

YLT - *The Young's Literal Translation Bible* (Public Domain).

OTHER HELPS:

Baxter, J. Sidlow (1960). *Awake My Heart*. Copyright © 1960. Zondervan Publishing Company, Grand Rapids, MI.

Blue, J. R. (1985). James. (J. F. Walvoord & R. B. Zuck, Eds.)*The Bible Knowledge Commentary: An Exposition of the Scriptures*. Wheaton, IL: Victor Books.

Chambers, Oswald (1935). Original edition © 1935. *My Utmost For His Highest*. Dodd, Mead & Company, Inc., New York, NY.

Jamieson, R., Fausset, A. R., & Brown, D. (1871). *Commentary Critical and Explanatory on the Whole Bible*. (Public Domain).

Keil, C. F., & Delitzsch, F. (1996). *Commentary on the Old Testament*. Peabody, MA: Hendrickson.

Peterson, Eugene H. (2007). *Conversations: THE MESSAGE with It's Translator*. Copyright © 2007 by Eugene H. Peterson. All rights reserved. THE MESSAGE Numbered Edition copyright © 2005. NavPress Publishing Group, Colorado Springs, CO.

Rohr, Richard. *Adam's Return: The Five Promises of Male Initiation*. Copyright © 2004. Crossroad Publishing Company, New York, NY. Used with permission.

Rohr, Richard. Preparing for Christmas: Daily Meditations for Advent. Copyright © 2008. Franciscan Media, Cincinnati, OH. Used with permission.

Rohr, Richard and Feister, John. *Radical Grace: Daily Meditations by Richard Rohr*. Copyright © 1995. St. Anthony Messengers Press, Cincinnati, OH. Used with permission.

Ryrie, Charles Caldwell (1995). *The Ryrie Study Bible, New American Standard*: with introductions, annotations, outlines, marginal references, harmony of the Gospels, synopsis of Bible doctrine, index of Scripture, index to notes, concordance, maps, and timeline charts, and many other helps. Expanded edition. Scripture taken from the NEW AMERICAN STANDARD BIBLE®, Copyright© 1960, 1962, 1963, 1968, 1971, 1972, 1973, 1975, 1994 by the Lockman Foundation. Used by permission.

Strong, J. (2009). *A Concise Dictionary of the Words in the Greek Testament and The Hebrew Bible*. Bellingham, WA: Logos Bible Software.

Thomas, R. L. (1998). *New American Standard Hebrew-Aramaic and Greek dictionaries : updated edition*. Anaheim: Foundation Publications, Inc.

Thomas, R. L., The Lockman Foundation. (1998). *New American Standard exhaustive concordance of the Bible: updated edition*. Anaheim: Foundation Publications, Inc.

ACKNOWLDEGEMENTS

I would be remiss if I didn't thank some people. Patti Paschall, the love of my life, is the one who prodded me the most to start putting my thoughts on paper. For over 35 years, she's been the one to lead the charge to encourage me. No one has believed in me more. Her "I love this" has been quite the life source. She is my Jesus with skin. She has everything to do with my finishing this project. I can't imagine such a venture without her being beside me. My one, my only, my queen. xo

My children and grandchildren also provide the most amazing motivation to spill the goods. My girls and their guys are spiritually very serious and engaged. They're on the edge, and they push me to peak over their ledge from time to time. I love their views. Nicole, Steve, Paige, and Jon: I could not be more blessed by you. xo

One thought that really helped me chill out and be real was the idea that one day my grandbabies will be Kingdom fire-breathers. They'll be much more aggressive in the Spirit than myself, but maybe there is enough here to feed them for a season or two. Isabel Rose, Jones Michael, Lewis Christian, Grace Irene, and those to follow: you are perfection in my heart! xo

I wrote and compiled the first month of devos in January 2010 and presented them to 18 of my intimate peers. I asked them for honest feedback. A few did indeed respond, but the majority never said a word. To those few who did respond, I got some major encouragement. Thank you.

In fact, it was my son-in-law, Jon, who drove the decisive nail when he asked me, *"Ba, who is your audience?"* Baaamm! I knew this project wasn't necessarily going to be for "church people." Anyone was welcome to read it, and I was totally fine with that, but the people Patti and I were mentoring as we traveled the globe were the audience that pulled on my heart. I wanted to talk to young men and women who were not hung up in some sort of religious system. From that point on, it was game on. Whether or not I accomplished that with this devo is yet to be seen.

I had a group of people I called the "Devo Club," who read the stuff I was emailing them weekly. Their faces were the ones I pictured when I was writing. Some of them periodically commented and offered suggestions. All of them encouraged me to keep going forward. Taryn Mast, Rocio Doyle, Darci Simpson, Jennifer Goeddertz, Megan Dietrich, Sara Hansen, Dennis Gable, Sarah Lapp Clements, Ashley Higgins, Erika Baldwin, and Kellen Gorbett. Thanks guys! I love you people dearly!

But there were two other members of the Devo Club who gave me feedback on a daily basis. Kayla and Andrea journaled their responses to each day's lesson and basically allowed me to peek into their hearts as they were processing the material. I can't even begin to explain how that kept me going!

Kayla Phillips Hindes was the voice of an angel. She reeks of encouragement anyway, but she really honed her craft when I needed it the most! Thanks baby. I'll owe you forever.

Andrea Gosselin jumped in during the editing process. She made her deeply vulnerable thoughts available to me on a daily basis. What a gift you are, woman! I love what you have with the Lord!

I have had two editors with this project, Erika and David. Erika Baldwin is a true spiritual daughter, but also an amazing wife to Bradley and a committed mother to Hannah and Luke. What it cost her to edit this project is a debt I'll never be able to repay. The Lord spoke clearly to me that she was to be my editor long before I asked her. Patti and I prayed hard about it. We knew this would be a drain on her family. Erika and I were in constant communication throughout the process—a time I'll always cherish. She was perfect for me. She clarified my scribbling without me having to lose my voice. That was what I wanted. That is what I got. Thanks babe! Love you! xo

David Reyes is a busy man. Too busy actually, but he volunteered to be the final eyes before we published ***RAW TALKS WITH WISDOM – Not Your Grandma's Devo***. His gorgeous wife Catherine (now carrying twins) and precious daughter Liv have patiently shared their David throughout this effort. David is a good son. He's served when he really didn't have the time or energy to do it. I'm grateful for his love and devotion. Thanks dude! xo

Once we decided to test readership with an email version of ***RAW TALKS WITH WISDOM – Not Your Grandma's Devo***, it simply would not have happened without Allison Johnston. She basically said, "I'll handle it," and that is exactly what she did. Allison would disappear for a week and then show up and say, "Look at this!" It was awesome! She also took all the pictures we used in the email version. She is the epitome of a spiritual daughter. Perfection really. Love you so much. xo

Jon Egan (my son by marriage) massaged the pics to make the images what we needed them to be. He's the one that has produced most of the graphics and set the overall ambience for the project. He also designed the cover and the Title Page. Again, he just fixed stuff. He always does. What a gift you are to God's people and to me. xo

And then there are the thousands of people who have allowed Patti and I to speak into their lives. I know what I know, and have learned what I have learned, because people were willing to ask me what I thought, and then give me space in their lives to work it out with them.

As I spoke, ministered, discipled, pastored, mentored, and tried to love, I learned a lot about people and probably even more about myself. Even when the stuff coming out of my mouth wasn't too good, most have loved on me well throughout the seasons. I do not deserve all the ways in which I have been honored. Not in the least. Thank you for your trust. I love you all.

And Lord, thank you for your patience, mercy, and unfailing love. You've changed me... from the inside out.

Thank you for everything! I am a blessed man!

Mike
2013

AUTHOR

Mike Paschall was born in Pine Bluff, Arkansas, but raised in Texas. He is a graduate of the University of Arkansas-Fayetteville with a BSEd. He also graduated from Southwestern Baptist Theological Seminary in Ft. Worth, Texas with an MDiv. Mike has served as pastor at numerous churches since 1987 and currently serves as pastor in the United Methodist Church. Mike and Patti were married in 1977. They have two daughters (Nicole, married to Steven Brewer, and Paige, married to Jon Egan) and six grandchildren (Isabel Rose, Jones Michael, Lewis Christian, Grace Irene, Esther Jane, and William Michael) who all live in Colorado Springs, CO. Mike loves any opportunity to mentor young pastors, missionaries, men and women who are passionate about ministry and Kingdom. He also loves preaching, teaching, and writing about the things of God. He is also particularly fond of a good hang with family, a cigar with a great friend, his Indian motorcycle, and an occasional trip to the golf course.

"David once told his son, Solomon, "Wisdom is the principle thing." I think every son craves a father that knows and lives that truth. Mike has taken me (and so many others) under his wing as a son and daily allowed me to grow by experiencing his wisdom, which was earned through all types of joys and sorrows. Wisdom IS the principle thing, and Mike models that by the way he lives, leads, shares and writes!" David Brown - Minister to Youth, Bella Vista Baptist Church, Bella Vista, AR.

"This devo is made most powerful by the man that lives the words every day. Mike Paschall's insights are a testament to a life worth the journey. More than a collection of daily readings—but a lifetime of wisdom, love, and challenge poured onto these pages. RAW TALKS WITH WISDOM will provoke you, inspire you, and make you scratch your head a bit. Often challenging the status quo that was lodged in my spirit, this devo led me to examine fully, wonder longer, and love deeper." - Allison Johnston - COO at Umba "an e-commerce platform for handmade goods," Atlanta, GA.

"Paschall is one of my best friends. Actually more than that, he's my priest. It's usually to him I go when I need a safe place to land my failures. I normally find brutal truth dripping with amazing grace. Regarding this book, it's become one my favorite daily meditations. Mike writes like he lives - vulnerable, honest, and real. WARNING, this book isn't for the staunchly,

overly religious, or spiritual know-it-alls. It's a devotional for regular folks, just like us..." Michael Hindes - coach, teacher, trainer, father, President of Kingdom Inc. & MRH Consulting, Atlanta, GA.

"Real, Raw, Biblical, Wise - did I say Raw? Yep - a lot like Mike, is this daily devo he's written, and it's what I love about it (and him). I've known Mike for over 25 years, and one of the things you can count in from him is that he'll tell it to ya straight - no song and dance - no shifting shadows - no wondering "what did he mean by that?" What's best, however, is that his straight talk comes from a place of wisdom, knowledge, experience, and love. There are few people in the planet whose opinion I value more, so just subscribe to the damn devo and read it! Good stuff!" David Johnson – Sr. Pastor at Church of the Open Door, author of *The Subtle Power of Spiritual Abuse*, Maple Grove, MN.

"Mike Paschall is my friend... this Devo is a frank, edgy communication of truths from the heart of God. I love Mike because of his honesty and transparency. If Jesus were talking to his disciples, or to the people of the day, I think he would smile at the conversational communications of this son. If you want a normal religious devotional reading, there are many available... but for those that have embarked on an honest difficult journey with a living Christ... I recommend Mike's Devo's... they will leave you thinking, crying, laughing and challenged." Dr. Bob Nichols - pastoral coach, counselor, teacher, Bellingham, WA

"Mike Paschall's mental and spiritual meanderings are thought provoking and interesting. Mike, who pastored mainstream churches in the past, presents a first hand account of religion, as some of us knew it, with a modern dose of common sense and the realization that all things change and deserve a re-look. Agree with Mike or not you will never be bored and his thoughts will cause you to think. Today's Christianity is due a new look and Christians owe it to themselves and others to use the critical thinking skills God gave us all." Rev. Paula Brown - A true West Texas girl, political purveyor, and forever poster-child of the 60's, Moody, TX.

"If it is real bread from God you want you have picked up the right book. Mike is a very real minister of the gospel that knows what you need when you wake up and you are starving for God to give you a Word for your life. Mike will blast you in the heart with his unique gifted use of language. Mike is one of the most important friends I have in the world. I have known Mike for over twenty-five years as one of my accountability friends. When I need a word from God, in a language that can only come from the Holy Spirit, I call Mike. He is truly gifted with speaking a tongue that you will understand. His devotional guides will guide you to the throne of God." Bart McMillan – Business Chaplain, President of Life's Lesson's Ministries, Gainesville, GA.

"As someone who has rarely done daily devotions, I did not know if I would keep up or stick with it. I've done both, and have thoroughly enjoyed and benefited from these daily "nuggets" of wisdom. These writings are insightful and thought provoking. I look forward to my devotion time every day." David Taylor - Senior Academic Consultant at a large private university, married father-of-two, McGregor, TX.

"Mike's devotionals are open, honest and refreshing. But most of all they are unfiltered by the spirit of "religion" that has invaded so much of biblical teaching in the world today. His desire for us to know the real Jesus is apparent in all that is included in this work. Whether you are a committed follower of Jesus Christ or seeking in your spiritual journey, I recommend this book for you." Barry Strickland - Texas Director of New Wilderness Adventures, Lancaster, TX.

"One of the characteristics of Mike Paschall that I greatly respect is his direct approach. He has a gift for unpacking principles and truths from God's Word and putting them in down-to-earth and in-your-face words that make it impossible to wiggle away from their weightiness. In RAW TALKS WITH WISDOM, Mike shares a daily dose of truth, without the sugar coating, that will lead you to a deeper relationship with God." Stephanie Pridgen - Missionary Church Administrator for International Christian Assembly, Kiev, Ukraine.

"Nothing strikes of more importance to me than 'a real Christian' and by that I mean a raw, lay it out on the table, I've made mistakes, and this is who I am Christian. We are called to make disciples and I truly believe we can't do that until we are real with each other. And that is why RAW TALKS WITH WISDOM is truly amazing. They are as real and raw as it gets. I truly believe the "church" is afraid to talk that way, but through Mike and his devos I have been able to face obstacles that I can assure you are not pretty or clean, but that is life and thank God somebody like Mike is not afraid to speak right to the heart of what life is really all about!" Taryn Mast – Performance Coach, San Diego, CA.

"To know Mike is to love him dearly or not at all, mostly because he leaves very little margin for misunderstanding. RAW TALKS WITH WISDOM is beautiful for that very reason; it is a heartfelt journey through the book of Proverbs that will lead you gracefully into a deeper relationship with Wisdom. 'In The Pages' offers an opportunity for each reader to work through the details as their story collides with God's story through the scriptures. If you are looking for a devotional that will make you feel safe, this isn't it. If you're searching for a daily opportunity to be honest with yourself and with God, then dive in... just keep in mind, this isn't your grandma's devo!" Dennis Gable – A multi-faceted, uniquely gifted Kingdom communicator who lives with his

gorgeous wife and beautiful children in Phoenix, AZ.

www.ingramcontent.com/pod-product-compliance
Lightning Source LLC
Chambersburg PA
CBHW021951290426
44108CB00012B/1022